PENGUIN REFERENCE
The Meaning of Tingo

'A luscious list of linguistic one-liners that no self-respecting toilet in the land should be without'
Daily Express

'Extraordinary' *Sunday Times*, Books of the Year

'A collection / dictionary / glossary (that it's indefinable is one of its many strengths) of words from around the world which have bizarrely exact meanings ... both educational and entertaining, and very funny as well'
Independent on Sunday

'I love *The Meaning of Tingo*' Benjamin Zephaniah

'A pleasure to dip into' *Sunday Telegraph*

'An addictive book of quirky words and phrases from around the world' *Time Out*

'The must-have British stocking filler ... this book is a gem'
Economist

'I love this book ... al

adine

ABOUT THE AUTHOR

Adam Jacot de Boinod's interest in foreign languages was
first aroused when doing research for the BBC programme
QI and subsequently developed into a full-on *vokabulyu*
(Russian – passion for foreign words). While searching
through 280 dictionaries, 140 websites and numerous
books on language, he developed an undoubted *samlermani*
(Danish – mania for collecting), became close to being
fisselig (German – flustered to the point of incompetence)
and narrowly avoided *karoshi* (Japanese – death from overwork). He is now intending to *nglayap* (Indonesian – wander far from home with no particular purpose).

The Meaning of Tingo

and other Extraordinary Words from around the World

Adam Jacot de Boinod

PENGUIN BOOKS

PENGUIN BOOKS

Published by the Penguin Group
Penguin Books Ltd, 80 Strand, London WC2R ORL, England
Penguin Group (USA) Inc., 375 Hudson Street, New York, New York 10014, USA
Penguin Group (Canada), 90 Eglinton Avenue East, Suite 700, Toronto,
Ontario, Canada M4P 2Y3 (a division of Pearson Penguin Canada Inc.)
Penguin Ireland, 25 St Stephen's Green, Dublin 2, Ireland (a division of Penguin Books Ltd)
Penguin Group (Australia), 250 Camberwell Road, Camberwell, Victoria 3124, Australia
(a division of Pearson Australia Group Pty Ltd)
Penguin Books India Pvt Ltd, 11 Community Centre, Panchsheel Park,
New Delhi – 110 017, India
Penguin Group (NZ), cnr Airborne and Rosedale Roads, Albany,
Auckland 1310, New Zealand (a division of Pearson New Zealand Ltd)
Penguin Books (South Africa) (Pty) Ltd, 24 Sturdee Avenue,
Rosebank, Johannesburg 2196, South Africa

Penguin Books Ltd, Registered Offices: 80 Strand, London WC2R ORL, England

www.penguin.com

First published 2005
Published in paperback 2006
1

Copyright © Adam Jacot de Boinod, 2005
Illustrations copyright © Sandra Howgate, 2005
All rights reserved

The moral right of the authors has been asserted

Set in 8.75/13 pt Swift
Designed by Andrew Barker
Typeset by Rowland Phototypesetting Ltd, Bury St Edmunds, Suffolk
Printed in Great Britain by Clays Ltd, St Ives plc

Contents

Foreword

My interest in the quirkiness of foreign words was triggered when one day, working as a researcher for the BBC quiz programme *QI*, I picked up a weighty Albanian dictionary to discover that they have no fewer than twenty-seven words for eyebrows and the same number for moustache, ranging from **mustaqe madh**, or bushy, to a **mustaqe posht**, one which droops down at both ends.

My curiosity rapidly grew into a passion. I was soon unable to go

near a second-hand bookshop or library without seeking out the shelves where the foreign language dictionaries were kept. I would scour books in friends' houses with a similar need to 'pan for gold'. My collection of wonderful words with no equivalent in the English language grew even longer, and I started to make a shortlist of my favourites: **nakhur**, for example, is a Persian word (which may not even be known to most native speakers) meaning 'a camel that won't give milk until her nostrils have been tickled'; and **areodjarekput**, the Inuit for 'to exchange wives for a few days only'. Many described strange or unbelievable things. When and why, for example, would a man be described as a **marilopotes**, Ancient Greek for 'a gulper of coaldust'? And could the Japanese samurai really have used the verb **tsuji-giri**, meaning 'to try out a new sword on a passer-by'?

Others expressed concepts that seemed all too familiar. We have all met a **Zechpreller**, the German description of 'someone who leaves without paying the bill'; spent too much time with an **ataoso**, Central American Spanish for 'one who sees problems with everything'; or worked with a **neko-neko**, Indonesian for 'one who has a creative idea which only makes things worse'.

My passion became a quiet obsession. I combed through over two million words in hundreds of dictionaries. I trawled the Internet, phoned Embassies, and tracked down foreign language speakers who could confirm my findings. I discovered that not everything sounds the same the world over: in Afrikaans, frogs go **kwaak-kwaak**, in Mexico cats go **tlatzomia**, while in Germany the noise of Rice Crispies' snap, crackle and popping is **Knisper! Knasper! Knusper!**

I found beautiful words to describe things for which we have no concise expression in English, like **serein**, the French for 'the rain that falls from a cloudless sky'; or **wamadat**, Persian for 'the intense heat of a sultry night'. I found words for all stages of life, from **paggiq**, Inuit for 'the flesh torn when a woman delivers a baby', through **Torschlusspanik**, German for 'the fear of diminishing opportunities as one gets older', to **mingmu**, Chinese for 'to die without regret'. I savoured the direct logic of Danish, the succinctness of Malay, the sheer wackiness of Japanese, and realized that sometimes a dictionary can tell you more about a culture than a guidebook.

I looked at languages from all corners of the world, from the Fuegian of southernmost Chile to the Inuit of northernmost Alaska, and from the Maori of the remote Cook Islands to Siberian Yakut. Some of them describe, of course, strictly local concepts and sensations, such as the Hawaiian **kapau'u**, 'to drive fish into the waiting net by striking the water with a leafy branch'; or **pukajaw**, Inuit for 'firm snow that is easy to cut and provides a warm shelter'. But others reinforce the commonality of human experience. Haven't we all felt **termangu-mangu**, Indonesian for 'sad and not sure what to do' or **mukamuka**, Japanese for 'so angry one feels like throwing up'? Most reassuring is to find the thoughts that lie on the tip of an English tongue, here crystallized into vocabulary: from the Zambian language of Bemba **sekaseka**, 'to laugh without reason', through the Czech **nedovtipa**, 'one who finds it difficult to take a hint', to the Japanese **bakku-shan**, 'a woman who appears pretty when seen from behind but not from the front'.

The English language has a long-established and voracious tendency to naturalize the best foreign words: **ad hoc**, **feng shui**, **croissant**, **kindergarten**. We've been pinching words from other cultures for centuries. Here are some we missed. I hope you enjoy them as much as I do.

Adam Jacot de Boinod

I've done my best to check the accuracy of all the terms but if you have any suggestions for changes (and, of course, I'd love to know of your own favourite foreign words) do please send them in to my website: **www.themeaningoftingo.com**.

Acknowledgements

I am deeply grateful to the following people for their advice and help: Giles Andreae, Martin Bowden, David Buckley, Candida Clark, Anna Coverdale, Nick Emley, Natasha Fairweather, William Hartston, Beatrix Jacot de Boinod, Nigel Kempner, Nick and Galia Kullmann, Alf Lawrie, John Lloyd, Sarah McDougall, Yaron Meshoulam, Tony Morris, David Prest, David Shariatmadari and Christopher Silvester.

In particular I must thank my agent, Peter Straus; my illustrator Sandra Howgate; my excellent editorial team at Penguin, Nigel Wilcockson, Georgina Laycock and Sophie Lazar; and Mark McCrum for his invaluable work on the text.

Meeting and Greeting

ai jiao de maque bu zhang rou
(Chinese)
*sparrows that love to chirp won't put on
weight*

¡Hola!

The first and most essential word in all languages is surely 'hello', the word that enables one human being to converse with another:

aa (Diola, Senegal)
beeta (Soninke, Mali, Senegal and Ivory Coast)
bok (Croatian)
boozhoo (Ojibwe, USA and Canada)
daw-daw (Jutlandish, Denmark)
ella (Awabakal, Australia)
i ay (Huaorani, Ecuador)
khaumykhyghyz (Bashkir, Russia)
nark (Phorhépecha, Mexico)
rozhbash (Kurdi, Iraq and Iran)
samba (Lega, Congo)
wali-wali (Limbe, Sierra Leone)
xawaxan (Toltichi Yokuts, California, USA)
yoga (Ateso, Uganda)
yoyo (Kwakiutl, Canada)

But it may not even be a word. In the Gilbert Islands of the Pacific, **arou pairi** describes the process of rubbing noses in greeting. For the Japanese, bowing is an important part of the process and a sign

of respect: **ojigi** is the act of bowing; **eshaku** describes a slight bow (of about 15 degrees); **keirei**, a full bow (of about 45 degrees); while **saikeirei** is a very low, worshipful type of bow that involves the nose nearly touching the hands. When one meets someone extremely important, one might even consider **pekopeko**, bowing one's head repeatedly in a fawning or grovelling manner.

Just say the word

Sometimes a single word works hard. In Sri Lanka, for example, the Sinhala word **ayubowan** means not only 'good morning', but also 'good afternoon', 'good evening', 'good night' and 'goodbye'.

Expectant

The frustration of waiting for someone to turn up is beautifully encapsulated in the Inuit word **iktsuarpok**, meaning 'to go outside often to see if someone is coming'. As for the frustration of the caller, there's always the Russian **dozvonit'sya** which doesn't simply mean to ring a doorbell, but to ring it until one gets an answer (it's also used for getting through on the telephone).

Hey you!

Once the first encounter is out of the way the correct form of address is important. Most of us know the difference between the intimate French **tu** and the more impersonal (and polite) **vous**. A similar distinction exists in Arabic between **anta** ('you' singular) and **antum** ('you' plural) – addressing an important person with **anta** (**anti** is the feminine version) rather than **antum** would be considered impolite.

In Vietnam there are no fewer than eighteen words for 'you', the use of which depends on whom you are addressing, whether a child or a senior citizen, whether formally or informally. And in the Western Australian Aboriginal language of Jiwali there are four words for 'we': **ngali** means 'we two including you'; **ngaliju** means 'we two excluding you'; **nganthurru** means 'we all including you'; and **nganthurraju** means 'we all excluding you'.

Cripes!

Exclamations are generally used to express a sudden reaction: to something frightening, incredible, spectacular, shocking or wonderful. Best not attempted by the visitor, they are better heard from the mouth of the native speaker than read off the page:

aaberdi (Algerian) a cry used when learning fearful news
aawwaah (Dardja, Algeria) a shout of doubt or hesitation
aăx (Karuk, North America) how disgusting!
aduh (Malay) ouch or wow!
aduhai (Indonesian) an expression of admiration
alaih (Ulwa, Nicaragua) gosh! goodness! help!
alalau (Quechuan, Peru) brrr! (of cold)
amit-amit (Indonesian) forgive me!

ammazza (Italian) it's a killer! wow!

asshe (Hausa, Nigeria) a cry of grief at distressing news

bambule (Italian) cheers! (preceding the lighting of a joint)

cq (Albanian) a negative exclamation of mild disappointment

hoppla (German) whoops!

naa (Japanese) that's great!

nabocklish (Irish Gaelic) don't meddle with it!

oho (Hausa, Nigeria) I don't care

oop (Ancient Greek) a cry to make rowers stop pulling

sa (Afrikaans) catch him!

savul (Turkish) get out of the way!

schwupp (German) quick as a flash

shahbash (Anglo-Indian) well done! (or well bowled!, as said in cricket by a wicket-keeper to the bowler)

tao (Chinese) that's the way it goes

taetae tiria (Cook Islands Maori) throw it away, it's dirty!

uf (Danish) ugh! yuk!

usch då (Swedish) oh, you poor thing!

y-eazziik (Dardja, Algeria) an expression used exclusively by women to criticize another person's action

zut (French) dash it!

Chinwag

The niceties of what in English is baldly known as 'conversation' are well caught in other languages:

ho'oponopono (Hawaiian) solving a problem by talking it out

samir (Persian) one who converses at night by moonlight

begadang (Indonesian) to stay up all night talking

glossalgos (Ancient Greek) talking till one's tongue aches

Breakdown in communication

Whether the person you are talking to suffers from **latah** (Indonesian), the uncontrollable habit of saying embarrassing things, or from **chenyin** (Chinese), hesitating and muttering to oneself, conversation may not always be quite as we'd like it:

catra patra (Turkish) the speaking of a language incorrectly and brokenly

nyelonong (Indonesian) to interrupt without apology

akkisuitok (Inuit) never to answer

dui niu tanqin (Chinese) to talk over someone's head or address the wrong audience (literally, to play the lute to a cow)

'a'ama (Hawaiian) someone who speaks rapidly, hiding their meaning from one person whilst communicating it to another

dakat' (Russian) to keep saying yes

dialogue de sourds (French) a discussion in which neither party listens to the other (literally, dialogue of the deaf)

mokita (Kiriwana, Papua New Guinea) the truth that all know but no one talks about

Tittle-tattle

Gossip – perhaps more accurately encapsulated in the Cook Island Maori word **'o'onitua**, 'to speak evil of someone in their absence' – is a pretty universal curse. But it's not always unjustified. In Rapa Nui (Easter Island) **anga-anga** denotes the thought, perhaps groundless, that one is being gossiped about, but it also carries the sense that this may have arisen from one's own feeling of guilt. A more gentle form of gossip is to be found in Jamaica, where the patois word **labrish** means not only gossip and jokes, but also songs and nostalgic memories of school.

False friends

Those who learn languages other than their own will sometimes come across words which look or sound the same as English, but mean very different things. Though a possible source of confusion, these false friends (as linguists call them) are much more likely to provide humour – as any Englishwoman who says 'bless' to her new Icelandic boyfriend will soon discover:

hubbi (Arabic) friendly

kill (Arabic) good friend

bless (Icelandic) goodbye

no (Andean Sabela) correct

aye (Amharic, Ethiopia) no

fart (Turkish) talking nonsense

machete (Aukan, Suriname) how

The unspeakable ...

Cursing and swearing are practised worldwide, and they generally involve using the local version of a small set of words describing an even smaller set of taboos that surround God, the family, sex and the more unpleasant bodily functions. Occasionally, apparently inoffensive words acquire a darker overtone, such as the Chinese **wang bah dahn**, which literally means a turtle egg but is used as an insult for politicians. And offensive phrases can often be beguilingly inventive:

> **zolst farliren aleh tseyner achitz eynm, un dos zol dir vey ton** (Yiddish) may you lose all your teeth but one and may that one ache

> **así te tragues un pavo y todas las plumas se conviertan en cuchillas de afeitar** (Spanish) may all your turkey's feathers turn into razor blades

... the unmentionable

Taboo subjects, relating to local threats or fears, are often quirky in the extreme. Albanians, for example, never use the word for 'wolf'. They say instead **mbyllizogojen**, a contraction of a sentence meaning 'may God close his mouth'. Another Albanian taboo-contraction is the word for fairy, **shtozovalle**, which means may 'God increase their round-dances'. Similarly, in the Sami language of Northern Scandinavia and the Yakuts language of Russia, the original name for bear is replaced by a word meaning 'our lord' or 'good father'. In Russian itself, for similar reasons, a bear is called a **medved'** or 'honey-eater'.

... and the unutterable

In Masai the name of a dead child, woman or warrior is not spoken again and, if their name is also a word used every day, then it is no longer used by the bereaved family. The Sakalavas of Madagascar do not tell their own name or that of their village to strangers to prevent any mischievous use. The Todas of Southern India dislike uttering their own name and, if asked, will get someone else to say it.

Shocking soundalikes

The French invented the word **ordinateur**, supposedly in order to avoid using the first two syllables of the word computer (**con** is slang for vagina and **pute** for whore). Creek Indians in America avoid their native words for earth (**fakki**) and meat (**apiswa**) because of their resemblance to rude English words.

In Japan, four (**shi**) and nine (**ku**) are unlucky numbers, because the words sound the same as those for 'death' and 'pain or worry' respectively. As a result, some hospitals don't have the numbers 4, 9, 14, 19, or 42 for any of their rooms. Forty-two (**shi-ni**) means to die, 420 (**shi-ni-rei**) means a dead spirit and 24 (**ni-shi**) is double death. Nor do some hospitals use the number 43 (**shi-zan**), especially in the maternity ward, as it means stillbirth.

Fare well

Many expressions for goodbye offer the hope that the other person will travel or fare well. But it is not always said. **Yerdengh-nga** is a Wagiman word from Australia, meaning 'to clear off without telling anyone where you are going'. Similarly, in Indonesia, **minggat** means 'to leave home for good without saying goodbye'.

Snobs and chauffeurs

Words don't necessarily keep the same meaning. Simple descriptive words such as 'rain' or 'water' are clear and necessary enough to be unlikely to change. Other more complex words have often come on quite a journey since they were first coined:

al-kuhul (Arabic) originally, powder to darken the eyelids; then taken up by alchemists to refer to any fine powder; then applied in chemistry to any refined liquid obtained by distillation or purification, especially to alcohol of wine, which then was shortened to alcohol

chauffer (French) to heat; then meant the driver of an early steam-powered car; subsequently growing to chauffeur

An Arabian goodbye

In Syrian Arabic, goodbye is generally a three-part sequence: a) **bxatrak**, by your leave; b) **ma'assalama**, with peace; c) **'allaysallmak**, God keep you. If a) is said first, then b) is the reply and then c) may be used. If b) is said first, then c) is obligatory.

hashhashin (Arabic) one who smokes or chews hashish; came to mean assassin

manu operare (Latin) to work by hand; then narrowed to the act of cultivating; then to the dressing that was added to the soil, manure

prestige (French) conjuror's trick; the sense of illusion gave way to that of glamour which was then interpreted more narrowly as social standing or wealth

sine nobilitate (Latin) without nobility; originally referred to any member of the lower classes; then to somebody who despised their own class and aspired to membership of a higher one; thus snob

theriake (Greek) an antidote against a poisonous bite; came to mean the practice of giving medicine in sugar syrup to disguise its taste; thus treacle

From Top to Toe

chi non ha cervello abbia
gambe *(Italian)*
he who has not got a good brain
ought to have good legs

Use your onion ...

English-speakers are not the only ones to use food metaphors – bean, loaf, noodle, etc. – to describe the head. The Spanish **cebolla** means both 'head' and 'onion', while the Portuguese expression

cabeça d'alho xoxo literally means 'he has a head of rotten garlic' (in other words, 'he is crazy'). Moving from vegetables to fruit, the French for 'to rack your brains' is **se presser le citron** – 'to squeeze the lemon'.

... or use your nut

In Hawaii, a different item of food takes centre stage. The word **puniu** means 'the skull of a man which resembles a coconut'. Hawaiian has also given the world the verb **pana po'o**, 'to scratch your head in order to help you remember something you've forgotten'.

Pulling faces

The Arabic **sabaha bi-wajhi** means to begin the day by seeing some-one's face. Depending on their expression, this can be a good or bad omen:

> **sgean** (Scottish Gaelic) a wild look of fear on the face
>
> **kao kara hi ga deru** (Japanese) a blush (literally, a flame comes out of one's face)

> **verheult** (German) puffy-faced and red-eyed from crying
>
> **Backpfeifengesicht** (German) a face that cries out for a fist in it

Greek face-slapping

There are several vivid Greek words for being slapped in the face, including **sfaliara**, **hastouki**, **fappa**, **xestrefti**, **boufla**, **karpasia** and **sulta'meremet** ('the Sultan will put you right'). **Batsos** means both 'a slap in the face' and 'a policeman' (from the American use of the word 'cop' to mean 'swipe'). **Anapothi** describes a backhanded slap, while **tha fas bouketo**, 'you will eat a bunch of flowers', is very definitely not an invitation to an unusual meal.

Windows of the soul

Eyes can be our most revealing feature, though the way others see them may not always be quite what we'd hoped for:

makahakahaka (Hawaiian) deep-set eyeballs
mata ego (Rapa Nui, Easter Island) eyes that reveal that a
   person has been crying
ablaq-chashm (Persian) having intensely black and white eyes
jegil (Malay) to stare with bulging eyes
melotot (Indonesian) to stare in annoyance with widened eyes

All ears

English is not terribly helpful when it comes to characterizing ears, unlike, say, Albanian, in which people distinguish between **veshok** ('small ones') or **veshak** ('ones that stick out'). Other languages are similarly versatile:

tapawising (Ulwa, Nicaragua) pointed ears
a suentola (Italian) flappy ears
mboboyo (Bemba, Congo and Zambia) sore ears

Indonesian offers two useful verbs: **nylentik**, 'to flick someone with the middle finger on the ear', and **menjewer**, 'to pull someone by the ear'. While the Russian for 'to pull someone's leg' is **veshat' lapshu na ushi**, which literally translates as 'to hang noodles on someone's ears'.

A real mouthful

In Nahuatl, the language of the Aztecs which is still spoken today in Mexico, **camachaloa** is 'to open one's mouth', **camapaca** is 'to wash one's mouth', and **camapotoniliztli** is 'to have bad breath'.

Getting lippy

Lips can be surprisingly communicative:

zunda (Hausa, Nigeria) to indicate with one's lips

catkhara (Hindi) smacking either the lips or the tongue against the palate

die beleidigte Leberwurst spielen (German) to stick one's lower lip out sulkily (literally, to play the insulted liver sausage)

ho'oauwaepu'u (Hawaiian) to stick the tongue under one's lip or to jut out the chin and twist the lips to the side to form a lump (as a gesture of contempt)

Hooter

Noses are highly metaphorical. We win by a nose, queue nose to tail or ask people to keep their noses out of our business. Then, if they are annoying us, it's that same protuberant feature we seize on:

irgham (Persian) rubbing a man's nose in the dirt

hundekuq (Albanian) a bulbous nose, red at the tip

nuru (Roviana, Solomon Islands) a runny nose

engsang (Malay) to blow the nose with your fingers

ufuruk (Turkish) breath exhaled through the nose

Albanian face fungus

Just below the nose may be found a feature increasingly rare in this country, but popular amongst males in many other societies. In Albania the language reflects an interest bordering on obsession, with no fewer than twenty-seven separate expressions for this fine addition to the upper lip. Their word for moustache is similar to ours (**mustaqe**) but once attached to their highly specific adjectives, things move on to a whole new level:

madh bushy moustache

holl thin moustache

varur drooping moustache

big handlebar moustache

kacadre moustache with turned-up ends

glemb moustache with tapered tips

posht moustache hanging down at the ends

fshes long broom-like moustache with bristly hairs

dirs ur newly sprouted moustache (of an adolescent)

rruar with the moustache shaved off

... to name but ten. The attention the Albanians apply to facial hair they also apply to eyebrows, with another twenty-seven words, including pencil-thin (**vetullkalem**), frowning (**vetullvrenjtur**), plucked (**vetullhequr**), knitted (**vetullrrept**), long and delicately shaped (**vetullgajtan**), thick (**vetullor**), joined together (**vetullperpjekur**), gloomy (**vetullngrysur**), or even arched like the crescent moon (**vetullhen**).

Bearded wonder

The Arab exclamation 'God protect us from hairy women and beardless men' pinpoints the importance of facial hair as a mark of rank, experience and attractiveness:

gras bilong fes (Tok Pisin, Papua New Guinea) a beard
   (literally, grass belonging to the face)
hemigeneios (Ancient Greek) with only half a beard
qarba (Persian) white hairs appearing in the beard
sim-zanakh (Persian) with a silver chin
poti (Tulu, India) a woman with a beard

False friends

willing (Abowakal, Australia) lips
buzz (Arabic) nipple
bash (Zulu) head
thumb (Albanian) teat
finger (Yiddish) toe

Bad hair day

Hair on the top of the head – or the lack of it – remains a worldwide preoccupation:

basribis (Ulwa, Nicaragua) having uneven, poorly cut hair
daberlack (Ullans, Northern Ireland) seaweed or
uncontrollable long hair
kudpalu (Tulu, India) a woman with uncombed hair
kucir (Indonesian) a tuft left to grow on top of one's otherwise
bald head

. . . not forgetting the Indonesian word **didis**, which means 'to search and pick up lice from one's own hair, usually when in bed at night'.

Teething troubles

Why doesn't English have an expression for the space between the teeth when Malay does – **gigi rongak**? And that's not the only gap in our dental vocabulary:

mrongos (Indonesian) to have ugly protruding upper teeth
angil (Kapampangan, Philippines) to bare the fangs like a dog
laglerolarpok (Inuit) the gnashing of teeth
kashr (Persian) displaying the teeth in laughter
zhaghzhagh (Persian) the chattering of the teeth from the cold
or from rage

And that one bizarre word that few of us are ever likely to need:

puccekuli (Tulu, India) a tooth growing after the eightieth
year

Getting it in the neck

Although there are straightforward terms for the throat in almost all languages, it's when it comes to describing how the throat is used that things get interesting:

nwik-ga (Wagiman, Australia) to have a tickle in the throat

ngaobera (Pascuense, Easter Island) a slight inflammation of the throat caused by screaming too much

berdaham (Malaysian) to clear the throat, especially to attract attention

kökochöka (Nahuatl, Mexico) to make gulping sounds

jarida biriqihi (Arabic) he choked on but couldn't swallow saliva (from excitement, alarm or grief)

o ka la nokonoko (Hawaiian) a day spent in nervous anticipation of a coughing spell

Armless in Nicaragua

In Ulwa, which is spoken in the eastern part of Nicaragua, no distinction is made between certain parts of the body. So, for example, **wau** means either a thigh or a leg, **ting** is an arm or a hand (and **tingdak** means missing an arm or a hand), **tingmak** is a finger or a thumb, **tibur** is either a wrist or an ankle, and **kungbas** means a beard, a moustache or whiskers.

Safe pair of hands

Other languages are more specific about our extremities and their uses:

sakarlasmak (Turkish) to become butterfingered

lutuka (Tulu, India) the cracking of the fingers

angushti za'id (Persian) someone with six fingers

zastrich' (Russian) to cut one's nails too short

meshetmek (Turkish) to wipe with the wet palm of one's hand

anjali (Hindi) hollowed hands pressed together in salutation

Legging it

Undue attention is put on their shapeliness but the bottom line is it's good to have two of them and they should, ideally, be the same length:

papakata (Cook Islands Maori) to have one leg shorter than the other

baguettes (French) thin legs (literally, chopsticks or long thin French loaves)

x-bene (Afrikaans) knock-knees

bulurin-suq (Persian) with thighs like crystal

Footloose

We don't always manage to put our best one forward:

zassledit' (Russian) to leave dirty footmarks
mencak-mencak (Indonesian) to stamp one's feet on the
ground repeatedly, getting very angry
eshte thike me thike (Albanian) to stand toenail to toenail
(prior to an argument)

Mind the gap

Several cultures have words to describe the space between or behind limbs: **irqa** (Khakas, Siberia) is the gap between spread legs, and **awawa** (Hawaiian) that between each finger or toe. While **jahja** in Wagiman (Australia) and **waal** in Afrikaans both mean the area behind the knee.

Skin deep

We describe it with just one word but other cultures go much further, whether it's **alang** (Ulwa, Nicaragua), the fold of skin under the chin; **aka'aka'a** (Hawaiian), skin peeling or falling off after either sunburn or heavy drinking; or **karelu** (Tulu, India), the mark left on the skin by wearing anything tight. Another Ulwa word, **yuputka**, records something we have all experienced – having the sensation of something crawling on one's skin.

Covering up

Once it comes to adding clothes to the human frame, people have the choice of either dressing up . . .

tiré à quatre épingles (French) dressed up to the nines
(literally, drawn to four pins)

'akapoe (Cook Islands Maori) donning earrings or putting
flowers behind the ears

angkin (Indonesian) a long wide cloth belt worn by women to
keep them slim

Pomadenhengst (German) a dandy (literally, a hair-cream
stallion)

FHCP (French) acronym of **Foulard Hermès Collier Perles**,
Hermes scarf pearl necklace (a female Sloane Ranger)

or down . . .

opgelozen (Yiddish) a careless dresser

padella (Italian) an oily stain on clothes (literally, a frying pan)

Krawattenmuffel (German) one who doesn't like wearing ties

cotisuelto (Caribbean Spanish) one who wears the shirt tail
outside of the trousers

tan (Chinese) to wear nothing above one's waist

or just as they feel . . .

sygekassebriller (Danish) granny glasses

rash (Arabic) skirt worn under a sleeveless smock

alyaska (Russian) anorak or moon-boots

hachimaki (Japanese) headbands worn by males to encourage
concentration and effort

ujut'a (Quechuan, Peru) sandals made from tyres

English clothing

English words for clothes have slipped into many languages. Sometimes the usage is fairly literal, as in **smoking** to describe a dinner jacket in Swedish or Portuguese; or **pants** for a tracksuit in Spanish. Sometimes it's more metaphorical: the Hungarians call jeans **farmer**, while their term for a T-shirt is **polo**. In Barbados the cloth used for the lining of men's clothes is known as **domestic**. Sometimes it's just an odd mix: the Danish for jeans, for example, is **cowboybukser**, while the Japanese **sebiro** means a fashionably cut suit, being their pronunciation of Savile Row, London's famous street of tailors.

Go whistle

On the tiny mountainous Canary Island of La Gomera there is a language called Silbo Gomero that uses a variety of whistles instead of words (in Spanish **silbar** means to whistle). There are four 'vowels' and four 'consonants', which can be strung together to form more than four thousand 'words'. This birdlike means of communication is thought to have come over with early African settlers over 2500 years ago. Able to be heard at distances of up to two miles, the **silbador** was until recently a dying breed. Since 1999, however, Silbo has been a required language in La Gomera schools.

The Mazateco Indians of Oaxaca, Mexico, are frequently seen whistling back and forth, exchanging greetings or buying and selling goods with no risk of misunderstanding. The whistling is not really a language or even a code; it simply uses the rhythms and pitch of ordinary speech without the words. Similar whistling languages have been found in Greece, Turkey and China, whilst other forms of wordless communication include the talking drums (**ntumpane**) of the Kele in Congo, the xylophones used by the Northern Chin of Burma, the banging on the roots of trees practised by the Melanesians, the yodelling of the Swiss, the humming of the Chekiang Chinese and the smoke signals of the American Indians.

Movers and Shakers

mas vale rodear que no ahogar
(*Spanish*)
better go about than fall into the ditch

Shanks's pony

There's much more to walking than simply putting one foot in front of the other:

> **berlenggang** (Indonesian) to walk gracefully by swinging one's hands or hips
>
> **aradupopini** (Tulu, India) to walk arm in arm or hand in hand
>
> **uitwaaien** (Dutch) to walk in windy weather for fun

> **murr-ma** (Wagiman, Australia) to walk along in the water searching for something with your feet
>
> **'akihi** (Hawaiian) to walk off without paying attention to directions

Walking in Zimbabwe

The Shona-speaking people of Zimbabwe have some very specialized verbs for different kinds of walking: **chakwaira**, through a muddy place making a squelching sound; **dowora**, for a long time on bare feet; **svavaira**, huddled, cold and wet; **minaira**, with swinging hips; **pushuka**, in a very short dress; **shwitaira**, naked; **sesera**, with the flesh rippling; and **tabvuka**, with such thin thighs that you seem to be jumping like a grasshopper.

Malaysian movements

The elegant Malaysians have a highly specialized vocabulary to describe movement, both of the right kind, as in **kontal-kontil**, 'the swinging of long earrings or the swishing of a dress as one walks', and the wrong, as in **jerangkang**, 'to fall over with your legs in the air'. Others include:

kengkang to walk with your legs wide apart
tenjack to limp with your heels raised
kapai to flap your arms so as to stay afloat
gayat feeling dizzy while looking down from a high place
seluk to put your hand in your pocket
bongkeng sprawling face down with your bottom in the air

Ups . . .

Sometimes our movements are deliberately athletic, whether this involves hopping on one leg (**vogget** in Cornish, **hinke** in Danish), rolling like a ball (**ajawyry** in the Wayampi language of Brazil), or something more adventurous:

angama (Swahili) to hang in mid-air
vybafnout (Czech) to surprise someone by saying boo
puiyarpo (Inuit) to show your head above water
povskakat' (Russian) to jump one after another
tarere (Cook Islands Maori) to send someone flying through the air
lele kawa (Hawaiian) to jump into the sea feet first

Lele kawa, of course, is usually followed by **curglaff**, Scottish dialect for the shock felt when plunging into cold water.

... and downs

But on other occasions there seems to be a banana skin waiting for us on the pavement:

blart (Ullans, Northern Ireland) to fall flat in the mud

lamhdanaka (Ulwa, Nicaragua) to collapse sideways (as when walking on uneven ground)

tunuallak (Inuit) slipping and falling over on your back while walking

kejeblos (Indonesian) to fall into a hole by accident

apismak (Turkish) to spread the legs apart and collapse

jeruhuk (Malay) the act of stumbling into a hole that is concealed by long grass

False friends

gush (Albanian) to hug each other around the neck

shagit (Albanian) to crawl on one's belly

snags (Afrikaans) during the night

sofa (Icelandic) sleep

purr (Scottish Gaelic) to headbutt

What-d'you-call-it

Just because there is no word for it in English doesn't mean we haven't done it or experienced it:

mencolek (Indonesian) touching someone lightly with one finger in order to tease them

wasoso (Hausa, Nigeria) to scramble for something that has been thrown

idumbulu (Tulu, India) seizing each other tightly with both hands

přesezený (Czech) being stiff from sitting in the same position too long

'alo'alo kiki (Hawaiian) to dodge the rain by moving quickly

honuhonu (Hawaiian) to swim with the hands only

engkoniomai (Ancient Greek) to sprinkle sand over oneself

tallabe (Zarma, Nigeria) to carry things on one's head without holding on to them

gagrom (Boro, India) to search for a thing below water by trampling

chonggang-chongget (Malay) to keep bending forward and then straightening (as a hill-climber)

When it all goes horribly wrong . . .

That sinking feeling, **puangi** (Cook Islands Maori), the sensation of the stomach dropping away (as in the sudden surge of a lift, plane, swing or a tossed boat), is something we know all too well, as are:

dokidoki (Japanese) rapid pounding heartbeats caused by worry or surprise

a'anu (Cook Islands Maori) to sit huddled up, looking pinched and miserable

nggregeli (Indonesian) to drop something due to nerves

bingildamak (Turkish) to quiver like jelly

. . . scarper

baotou shucuon (Chinese) to cover one's head with both hands and run away like a coward

achaplinarse (Spanish, Central America) to hesitate and then run away in the manner of Charlie Chaplin

Learning to relax

In some parts of the world relaxation doesn't necessarily mean putting your feet up:

ongkang-ongkang (Indonesian) to sit with one leg dangling down

naganaga (Rapa Nui, Easter Island) to squat without resting your buttocks on your heels

lledorweddle (Welsh) to lie down while propping yourself up with one elbow

karvat (Hindi) the side of the body on which one rests

Dropping off

Once we start relaxing, snoozing becomes an increasingly strong possibility. Both Danish, with **raevesøvn**, and Russian, with **vpol-glaza**, have a word to describe sleeping with one eye open, while other languages describe other similar states of weariness:

aiguttoa (Votic, Estonia) to yawn repeatedly

teklak-tekluk (Indonesian) the head bobbing up and down with drowsiness

utsura-utsura (Japanese) to fluctuate between wakefulness and being half asleep

utouto (Japanese) to fall into a light sleep without realizing it

tengkurap (Indonesian) to lie or sleep with the face downwards

kulubut (Kapampangan, Philippines) to go under the blanket

Out for the count

Having achieved the state the Japanese describe as **guuguu**, 'the sound of someone in a deep sleep accompanied by snoring', we can either have a good night . . .

bilita mpash (Bantu, Zaire) blissful dreams

altjiranga mitjina (Aranda, Australia) the timeless dimensions of dreams

ngarong (Dyak, Borneo) an adviser who appears in a dream and clarifies a problem

rêve à deux (French) a mutual dream, a shared hallucination

morgenfrisk (Danish) fresh from a good night's sleep

. . . or a bad one:

menceracan (Malay) to cry in one's sleep

kekau (Indonesian) to wake up from a nightmare

igau (Malay) to talk while trapped in a nightmare

kerinan (Indonesian) to oversleep until the sun is up

Back as forth

Whatever their length, words have provided excellent material for games from the earliest times. One of the more pleasing arrangements is the palindrome, which is spelt the same backwards as forwards, and can create some bizarre meanings:

neulo taas niin saat oluen (Finnish) knit again, so that you will get a beer

Nie fragt sie: ist gefegt? Sie ist gar fein (German) she
  never asks: has the sweeping been done? She is very
  refined

in girum imus nocte et consumimur igni (Latin) we
  enter the circle after dark and are consumed by fire

nipson anomemata me monan opsin (Ancient Greek)
  wash (off) my sins, not only my face (written on the
  edge of a well in Constantinople: NB the 'ps' is a
  transcription of the Greek letter ψ)

The Finns have three of the world's longest palindromic
words:

saippuakivikauppias a soapstone seller
saippuakuppinippukauppias a soap-cup trader
solutomaattimittaamotulos the result from a
  measurement laboratory for tomatoes

Getting Around

dalu tongtian, ge zou yi bian
(Chinese)
the highway comes out of one's mouth

Thumbing it

Some rides are free:

fara a puttanu (Icelandic) to hitchhike (literally, to travel on the thumb)

usqar (Khakas, Siberia) to take someone on the back of one's horse

radif (Persian) one who rides behind another on the same horse

menggonceng (Indonesian) to have a free ride usually on a friend's bike

plomo (Spanish, Central America) a bus passenger who is just on for the free ride (literally, a lead weight)

Others involve money . . .

ngetem (Indonesian) to stop (of a bus) longer than necessary at unauthorized points along the route to the terminus to look for more paying passengers

ngojek (Indonesian) to earn money by carrying a paying passenger on the rear seat of one's motorbike

. . . or getting your own transport:

essoreuse (French) a noisy motorbike (literally, spindryer)

Warmwassergeige (German) a souped-up motorcycle (literally, warm-water violin)

teplushka (Russian) a heated goods van used for carrying people

bottom-bottom wata wata (African Creole) a submarine

gung gung chi chuh (Chinese) a bus

vokzal (Russian) a railway station (named after Vauxhall in London)

voiture-balai (French) the last train or bus (literally, broom-vehicle as it sweeps up the latecomers)

Set of wheels

One particular form of transport is pre-eminent in the modern world: whether normal, or convertible (**spider** in Italian), or vintage (**oldtimer** in German). What lets most cars down, however, are the people driving them, be it the **viande paraguero** (Caribbean Spanish), the Sunday driver (literally, an umbrella stand); or the **Gurtmuffel** (German), someone who doesn't wear a seat belt. Then, of course, there's the way people drive:

sgasata (Italian) a sudden and violent acceleration

appuyer sur le champignon (French) to put one's foot down (literally, to stamp on the mushroom)

Geisterfahrer (German), a person driving on the wrong side of the road

Road rage

Hazards are all too common, whether in the car . . .

desgomarse (Caribbean Spanish) to have bad tyres

ulykkesbilen (Danish) an ill-fated car

Blechlawine (German) a huge traffic jam (literally, a sheet-metal avalanche)

matadero (Spanish, Central America) a car scrapheap (literally, a slaughterhouse)

. . . or out of it. The French have the most evocative expressions to describe both the reckless pedestrian – **viande à pneux**, meat for tyres, and the knock suffered by a cyclist – **l'homme au marteau**, literally, the man with the hammer.

Apache cars

The Apache people of the USA name the parts of cars to correspond to parts of the body. The front bumper is **daw**, the chin or jaw; the front fender is **wos**, the shoulder; the rear fender is **gun**, the arm and hand; the chassis is **chun**, the back; the rear wheel is **ke**, the foot. The mouth is **ze**, the petrol-pipe opening. The nose is **chee**, the bonnet. The eyes are **inda**, the headlights. The forehead is **ta**, the roof.

The metaphorical naming continues inside. The car's electrical wiring is **tsaws**, the veins. The battery is **zik**, the liver. The petrol tank is **pit**, the stomach. The radiator is **jisoleh**, the lung; and its hose, **chih**, the intestine. The distributor is **jih**, the heart.

False friends

punk (Japanese) flat tyre
chariot (French) trolley
rower (Polish) bicycle
fly (Danish) aeroplane

escape (Portuguese) car exhaust or gas leak
arrear (Spanish) to drive on
jam (Mongolian) road

Running on time

The Japanese have some fine vocabulary for trains: **gaton gaton** is an electric train; **gotongoton** describes trains rattling along; **shoo shoo po po** is the sound of a steam train; while **kang kang kang** is the noise of the level crossing. **Kakekomi-josha** describes all too vividly rushing onto a train to beat the closing doors, a common sight on Tokyo's underground.

Separatist

Many of the languages around the world are inter-related (for example, Spanish, French and Italian are all Latin languages), but by contrast, 'isolate languages' are those that do not appear to be related to any other at all. Some languages became isolate in historical times, after all their known relatives became extinct; the Piraha language, for example, spoken along a tributary of the Amazon, is the last surviving member of the Mura family of languages. Similar isolates include Burushaski, which is spoken in two Himalayan valleys; the Gilyak and Ket languages of Siberia; and Nivkh, a Mongolian language.

The Basque language Euskara is perplexing. It bears no resemblance at all to the languages of its surrounding countries. Some similarities with Georgian have made linguists think it could be related to languages from the Caucasus. Others have tried to relate it to non-Arabic languages from the north of Africa. A more likely hypothesis argues that Euskara developed where it is still spoken and has always been the language of the Basques, who were gradually surrounded by people speaking other unrelated languages.

It Takes All Sorts

gading yang tak retak *(Indonesian)*
there is no ivory that isn't cracked

Tolerant

When it comes to personality, some people seem to have been put on the planet to make life easier for everyone else:

cooperar (Spanish, Central America) to go along willingly with someone else to one's own disadvantage

abbozzare (Italian) to accept meekly a far from satisfactory situation

ilunga (Tshiluba, Congo) someone who is ready to forgive any abuse the first time, to tolerate it a second time, but never a third time

Flattering

Others take things too far:

vaseliner (French) to flatter (literally, to apply vaseline)

happobijin (Japanese) a beauty to all eight directions (a sycophant)

Radfahrer (German) one who flatters superiors and browbeats subordinates (literally, a cyclist)

Fawning

The Japanese have the most vivid description for hangers-on: **kingyo no funi**. It literally means 'goldfish crap' – a reference to the way that a fish that has defecated often trails excrement behind it for some time.

Egotists

Sweet-talking others is one thing; massaging your own ego can be another altogether:

echarse flores (Spanish) to blow your own trumpet (literally, to throw flowers to yourself)

il ne se mouche pas du pied (French) he has airs above his station (literally, he doesn't wipe his nose with his foot)

yi luan tou shi (Chinese) courting disaster by immoderately overestimating one's own strength (literally, to throw an egg against a rock)

tirer la couverture à soi (French) to take the lion's share, all the credit (literally, to pull the blanket towards oneself)

The awkward squad

But there are worse horrors than the merely conceited:

ataoso (Spanish, Central America) one who sees problems with everything

kibitzer (Yiddish) one who interferes with unwanted advice

nedovtipa (Czech) one who finds it difficult to take a hint

neko-neko (Indonesian) to have a creative idea which only makes things worse

mukzib (Persian) one who eggs on or compels another to tell a lie

iant (Serbian) an attitude of proud defiance, stubbornness and self-preservation, sometimes to the detriment of everyone else – or even oneself

er gibt seinen Senf dazu (German) one who always has something to say even if no one else cares (literally, he brings his mustard along)

Pariah

Some people are able to tough it out whatever happens, imposing their faults on others till the day they die. Others are more sensitive:

scrostarsi (Italian) to remove oneself as if one were a scab (to move or go away because one's presence is not desired)

ulaia (Hawaiian) to live as a hermit because of disappointment

panaphelika (Ancient Greek) to be deprived of all playmates

Lazybones

Others like to spend time alone for altogether different reasons:

kopuhia (Rapa Nui, Easter Island) someone who disappears instead of dedicating himself to his work

linti (Persian) someone who idles his day away lying under a tree

nubie yam (Waali, Ghana) a farmer who points to his farm but does little more (literally, finger farm)

gober les mouches (French) to stand by idly (literally, to gulp down flies)

zamzama (Arabic) to waft along in a relaxed style

goyang kaki (Indonesian) relaxing and enjoying oneself as problems are sorted out by others (literally, to swing one's legs)

kalincak-kelincok (Balinese, Indonesia) the back and forth, here and there or up and down of genuine drifting

Otherwise engaged

Some take idleness to another level:

luftmensch (Yiddish) an impractical dreamer having no definite business or income

viajou na maionese (Portuguese) to live in a dream world (literally, to travel in the mayonnaise)

nglayap (Indonesian) to wander far from home with no particular purpose

umudrovat se (Czech) to philosophize oneself into the madhouse

Situation vacant

Given that many outsiders think of the Japanese as a nation of workaholics, the language has an unusual number of verbs to describe different states of idleness: **boketto** is to gaze vacantly into space without thinking or doing anything; **bosabosa** is to sit around idly not doing what needs to be done; **gorogoro** is to spend time doing nothing (including lolling in a recumbent position); **guzuguzu** is to vacillate, procrastinate or to stretch out a job; while **bura-bura** is to wander around aimlessly, looking at the sights with no fixed destination in mind.

Manic obsessive

No one, as far as we know, died of laziness. Frantic activity, however, is another thing ...

Putzfimmel (German) a mania for cleaning
samlermani (Danish) a mania for collecting
Grüebelsucht (German) an obsession in which even the
simplest facts are compulsively queried
muwaswas (Arabic) to be obsessed with delusions
potto (Japanese) to be so distracted or preoccupied that you
don't notice what is happening right in front of you

... and can lead to **karoshi** (Japanese), death from overwork.

The German mindset

A distinguishing feature of the German language is its creation of evocative concepts by linking different words together, useful for depicting not just characters but states of mind. Most of us know **Schadenfreude** (literally, damage joy), which describes what we hardly dare express: that feeling of malicious pleasure in someone else's misfortune. But there are numerous others. We've all had a boss who's suffered from **Betriebsblindheit**: organizational blindness; and who has not worked alongside someone who is **fisselig**: flustered to the point of incompetence? That very same person could be described as a **Korinthenkacker**: one who is overly concerned with trivial details.

False friends

fatal (German) annoying

hardnekkig (Dutch) stubborn

lawman (Aukan, Suriname) crazy person

estúpido (Portuguese) rude

morbido (Italian) soft, tender

xerox (French) unoriginal or robotic individual

extravagans (Hungarian) eccentric

konsekvent (Swedish) consistent

Fools and rogues

There's a rich stream of invective running through the world's languages when it comes to people we regard as less intelligent than ourselves. The Cantonese equivalent to 'you're as thick as two short planks' is the equally graphic **nie hochi yat gau faan gam**, 'you look like a clump of cooked rice', while the German equivalent to 'not quite all there' is **nicht alle Tassen im Schrank haben**, 'not to have all the cups in the cupboard' (not to have all one's marbles).

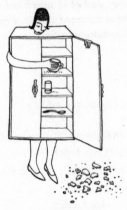

Meanwhile the Maoris of the Cook Islands have the telling word **varevare**, which means 'to be very young and still quite hopeless'.

Schlumps and schleppers

When it comes to insults, few languages can compete with Yiddish. In this wonderfully evocative language, a fool can be not just a **shmutte** or a **schlump** but a **nar**, a **tam**, a **tipesh**, a **bulvan**, a **shoyte**, a **peysi**, a **kuni lemel**, a **lekish**, or even a **shmenge**.

Not content with these, the language gets more specific. A loser is a **schlepper**, a **shmugeggeshnorrer**, a **paskudnik**, a **pisher**, a **yold** or even a **no-goodnik**. A **klutz** is a clumsy, oafish bungler and a **lekish ber schlemiel** is a fool without luck. A fool who is not just stupid but inept is a **schlimazl**. A **farshpiler** is one who has lost all his money gambling. The saddest of all is perhaps the **nisrof**, the burnt-out fool.

Other fine insults in Yiddish have included:

nebbish a nobody
nudnick a yakky, aggressively boring person
putz a simpleton
shlub a clumsy and ill-mannered person
shmegegge a foolish person and a sycophant
shmendrick a timid nonentity
shnook a nice but pathetic gullible person

All talk

Worse than the fool is one of those people who occur in every organization on the planet: the **buchipluma** (Caribbean Spanish), the person who promises but doesn't deliver. The same language has a useful verb for the way such people behave: **culipanear**, which means to look for excuses for not meeting obligations.

Fibbers

Even the infuriating **buchipluma** is surely preferable to the outright liar. And, as Japanese vividly shows, from lying to someone (**nimaijita o tsukau**, to use two tongues), it's just a small step to duping (**hanage o nuku handy**, literally, to pull the hair out of their nostrils) or doublecrossing them (**negaeri o utsu**, literally, to roll them over while sleeping).

Salt of the earth

What a shame that we can't all be uncomplicatedly good: for example, when you're acting with **meraki** (a Greek word) you're doing something with soul, creativity or love, and putting something of yourself into what you're doing:

tubli (Estonian) orderly, strong, capable, hard-working,
    persistent, productive, setting an example to others,
    behaving properly or having will power
ondinnonk (Iroquoian, USA) the soul's innermost benevolent
    desires or the angelic parts of human nature

Indonesian two in one

Indonesian has many words that combine two aspects of character or appearance into a single simple word. So you might well know someone who is **ricuh**, that is, chaotic and noisy; **pandir**, stupid, but innocent and honest; **mungil**, tiny and pretty; **merana**, lonely and miserable; **lencir**, slim and tall; **bangkot**, old and cantankerous; or **klimis**, smooth and shiny.

Tall poppies

Sweden is a country that not only values the concept of a lack of extremes but even has a word for it – **lagom**. In this society, it's generally not thought to be good to stand out too much. Everything and everyone is supposed to be just **lagom** – which is not to say 'boring', so much as 'not too much and not too little', 'not good and not bad', 'okay', 'just right', 'so-so'.

So so similar

The concept of 'so-so' is found in many languages, and often in a similarly repetitive form: it's **tako tako** in Bosnian/Croatian/Serbian, **aixi aixi** in Catalan, **cosi cosi** in Italian, **wale wale** in Chipewyan (Canada), **hanter hanter** in Cornish, **thik thik** in Gujarati (India), **hai hao** in Mandarin, **jako tako** in Polish, **ithin ithin** in Sinhala (Sri Lanka), **soyle boyle** in Turkish, **etsi ketsi** in Greek, **atal atal** in Occitan (France), **asina asina** in Asturian (Spain), **elae belae** in Azeri (Azerbaijan) and **azoy azoy** in Yiddish.

Happy talk

Good or bad, modest or conceited, hard-working or lazy, all of us experience the highs of emotion:

tout baigne dans l'huile (French) hunky-dory (literally, everything is bathing in oil)

ai bu shishou (Chinese) so delighted with something that one can scarcely take one's eyes off it

ichigo-ichie (Japanese) the practice of treasuring each moment and trying to make it perfect

pulaka (Tulu, India) hair that stands on end with ecstasy

bas-bhualadh (Scottish Gaelic) clapping one's hands from joy or grief

tuman (Indonesian) to find something enjoyable and want to have it again

mubshar (Persian) to be exhilarated with good news

zhuxing (Chinese) to add to the fun

Side-splitting

sekaseka (Bemba, Congo and Zambia) to laugh without reason

tergelak (Malay) laughing unintentionally

katahara itai (Japanese) laughing so much that one side of your abdomen hurts

Enraptured

The Japanese have particularly wonderful words for the deep joy that can come as a response to beauty: **uttori** is to be enraptured by the loveliness of something; **aware** describes the feelings created by ephemeral beauty; **yoin** is the reverberating sensation after the initial stimulus has ceased; while **yugen** goes further, describing an awareness of the universe that triggers feelings too deep and mysterious for words.

Down in the dumps

The causes of unhappiness are many, varied and not always easy to put your finger on:

termangu-mangu (Indonesian) sad and not sure what to do

mono-no-aware (Japanese) appreciating the sadness of existence

avoir le cafard (French) to be down in the dumps (literally, to have the cockroach)

litost (Czech) the state of torment created by the sudden realization of one's own misery

kusat' sebe lokti (Russian) to cry over spilt milk (literally, to bite one's elbows)

emakou (Gilbertese, Kiribati) a secret sorrow

bel hevi (Tok Pisin, Papua New Guinea) the heavy sinking feeling that often accompanies extreme sadness (literally, belly heavy)

Weltschmerz

Weltschmerz is another untranslatable German word. It broadly means world-weariness, but carries with it both a sense of sorrow at the evils of the world and a yearning for something better. Aspects of it can be found in the Welsh **hiraeth**, a mingled feeling of sadness, somewhere between homesickness and nostalgia, and the Portuguese **saudade**, the longing for things that were or might have been. Nostalgia also lies at the heart of the Brazilian Portuguese word **banzo**, which describes a slave's profound longing for his African homeland.

In the slough of despond

There are various ways to deal with feelings of despair. Either you can take a philosophical view and try to avoid the Persian concept of **sanud**, that is, the exercise of the mind upon an unprofitable subject; or you can adopt the defeatist attitude inherent in the Indonesian word **jera**, which means 'so scared by a past experience that one will never want to do it again'. Or you can take refuge in **Kummerspeck**, a German word that describes the excess weight you will gain from emotion-related overeating (literally, grief bacon).

Seeing red

Therapists would suggest it's better out than in:

mukamuka (Japanese) feeling so angry one feels like throwing up

geragas (Malay) to comb one's hair in anger

feau (Samoan) to recall good deeds done when one is angry

Survival instincts

Even though some languages are vanishing, in a world less hospitable to aboriginal peoples and more swamped by English, this does not mean it's impossible to keep endangered languages alive. Mohawk, for instance, spoken by indigenous groups in Quebec, was in retreat until the 1970s, when it was first codified and then taught to children in schools. Welsh and Maori have both made a comeback with concerted official help; and Navajo (USA), Hawaiian and several languages spoken in remote parts of Botswana have been artifically revived.

Iceland has managed to keep alive its native tongue, even though it is spoken by no more than 275,000 people; and the ancient Nordic language of Faroese, thought to have been once spoken by the Vikings, was preserved from extinction by the Danish government, who even went as far as putting grammar hints and verb declensions on the sides of milk cartons.

A powerful political purpose is another force for reviving an old language. Resurgent nationalism helped bring Irish back from the Celtic twilight; while the establishment of the nation of Israel has turned Hebrew from a written language into a proudly spoken national tongue.

Falling in Love

nam gawa the wei woe lu yoe;
phung dang si yang they nang
yoe (*Dzongkha, Bhutan*)
*fun and pleasure are located below the
navel; dispute and trouble are also
found there*

The language of love

In English the language of love is, metaphorically speaking, a violent and disorientating one: we fall in love, are love struck and struggle to avoid heartbreak. It seems things are the same throughout the world:

harawata o tatsu (Japanese) to break one's heart (literally, to sever one's intestines)

coup de foudre (French) love at first sight (literally, a flash of lightning)

mune o kogasu (Japanese) to pine away (literally, to scorch one's chest)

tragado como media de cartero (Colombian Spanish) being hopelessly in love (literally, swallowed like a postman's sock)

The rules of attraction …

Physical beauty is often the starting point for love:

pichón (Caribbean Spanish) a handsome young man (literally, young pigeon)

qiubo (Chinese) the bright and clear eyes of a beautiful woman
mahj (Persian) looking beautiful after a disease
avoir la frite (French) to be in great shape (literally, to have the French fry)
magandang hinaharap (Tagalog, Philippines) nice breasts (literally, nice future)
dayadrsti (Hindi) compassionate eyes
kemayu (Indonesian) to act like a beauty

Sometimes the basic materials need a little assistance:

slampadato (Italian) a person who gets tanned with an infra-red lamp
zhengrong (Chinese) to tidy oneself up or to improve one's looks by plastic surgery

. . . and of repulsion

The Japanese have a particular word for a situation in which attraction is all too brief. **Bakku-shan** is a girl who appears pretty when seen from behind but not from the front.

Would like to meet

English is somewhat deficient in words that describe the very early moments of attraction. We need a word like **mamihlapinatapei**, from the Fuegian language found in Chile, meaning that shared look of longing where both parties know the score yet neither is willing to make the first move. Other, more active approaches include:

basabasa (Arabic) to ogle, make sheep's eyes, cast amorous
   glances
piropo (Spanish) a compliment paid on the street (which
   ranges from polite to raunchy)
xiyyet (Dardja, Algeria) he is sewing (this is said of someone
   who is trying to win over a girl, especially by talking)

pulir hebillas (Spanish, Central America) to polish belt
   buckles (to dance very closely)

The direct approach

The Italians are masters at taking matters to the next level: **pomicione** is a man who seeks any chance of being in close physical contact with a woman; **puntare** is to stare intensely at the one to whom one feels sexually attracted; while **tirino** is the sound made by smacking one's lips together like a loud kiss to indicate attraction. Sometimes a boy will say **cibi cierre** to a girl (**CBCR**). This is an acronym of **cresci bene che ripasso**: 'if you still look like that when you've grown up, I will come and pay you a call' . . .

Dîner à un

. . . while the French have perfected the art of rejection:

poser un lapin à quelqu'un to stand someone up (literally, to lay a rabbit on someone)

Saint-Glinglin a date that is put off indefinitely (**jusqu' à la Saint-Glinglin** means never in a month of Sundays)

Japanese dating

Rainen no kono hi mo issho ni waratteiyoh is one of the country's most successful chat-up lines; it means 'this time next year let's be laughing together'.

Commitment-phobe

The romantic ideal is **Einfühlungsvermögen**, the German word for an understanding so intimate that the feelings, thoughts and motives of one person are readily comprehended by the other; but the route to that happy state can so often be confused by the insincere:

biodegradabile (Italian) someone who falls in love easily and often

capkinlasmak (Turkish) to turn into a skirt chaser

leonera (Spanish, Central America) a bachelor pad (literally, a lion's den)

vieux marcheur (French) an elderly man who still chases women (literally, an old campaigner)

False friends

nob (Wolof, Gambia and Senegal) to love

city (Czech) feelings

dating (Chinese) to ask about, enquire

baron (French) sugar daddy

agony (Rasta Patois) sensations felt during sex

bonk (Afrikaans) lump or thump

song (Vietnamese) to live life

Affairs of the heart

When things can go so sweetly . . .

alamnaka (Ulwa, Nicaragua) to find one's niche, to meet a kindred soul

pelar la pava (Caribbean Spanish) to be alone romancing one's sweetheart (literally, to pluck a female turkey)

andare in camporella (Italian) to go into a secluded spot in the countryside to make love

hiza o majieru (Japanese) to have an intimate talk (literally, to mingle each other's knees)

queesting (Dutch) allowing a lover access to one's bed under the covers for chit-chat

ghalidan (Persian) to move from side to side as lovers, to roll, wallow or tumble

. . . how can they be so bitter at the end?

aki ga tatsu (Japanese) a mutual cooling of love (literally, the autumn breeze begins to blow)

razblyuto (Russian) the feeling for someone once but no longer loved

dejar con el paquete (Spanish) abandoning a woman one has made pregnant (literally, to drop with the parcel)

plaqué (French) dumped (literally, laid flat or rugby-tackled)

cavoli riscaldati (Italian) an attempt to revive a lapsed love affair (literally, reheated cabbage)

Reality check

The Boro people of India have a sophisticated understanding of the complexities of loving: **onsay** means to pretend to love; **ongubsy** means to love deeply, from the heart; and **onsia** signifies loving for the very last time.

Love for sale

Who better than the pragmatic French to construct a precise terminology for love as a business, ranging from a **passe raide**, the basic price for a sex session, to the **kangourou**, a prospective client who hesitates (hops around) before deciding on a girl. When it comes to those who ply their trade, there are many equally specific terms. An **escaladeuse de braguette** is, literally a zipper climber; a **beguineuse** is an unreliable prostitute; a **wagonnière** is a woman who solicits on trains; a **truqueur** means a rentboy who blackmails his clients; while a **cocotte-minute** is a pro who turns many tricks very quickly (literally, a pressure cooker). There is even an expression, **commencer à rendre la monnaie**, to show signs of age, which is said of prostitutes who in better days didn't have to give change for large notes.

Let's talk about sex

The Mosuo people in China have three sacred taboos: it's forbidden to eat dog, to eat cat and to talk about sex. The latter taboo doesn't seem to apply elsewhere:

avoir la moule qui bâille (French) to be horny (literally, to have a yawning mussel)

menggerumut (Indonesian) to approach somebody quietly in the night for sex

jalishgar (Persian) to be addicted to sexual intercourse

carezza (Italian) sexual intercourse in which ejaculation is avoided (literally, caressing or petting)

Penis dialogues

There are many ways to describe **le petit chauve au col roulé** (French), the little baldy in a turtleneck, and the respect with which he's treated:

narachastra prayoga (Sanskrit) men who worship their own sexual organ

enfundarla (Spanish) to put one's penis back in one's pants (or one's sword back in its sheath)

zakilpistola (Basque) a sufferer from premature ejaculation (literally, pistol prick)

koro (Japanese) the hysterical belief that one's penis is shrinking into one's body

camisa-de-venus (Brazilian Portuguese) a condom (literally, shirt of Venus)

The Tagalog speakers of the Philippines take things further with the **batuta ni Drakula** ('Dracula's nightstick'). Added sexual pleasure can be gained from **pilik-mata ng kambing** (goat's eyelashes) or **bulitas** (small plastic balls surgically implanted to enlarge the penises of young Filipinos).

Sex for one ...

The vocabulary is no less specialized when it comes to what the Italians describe as **assolo**, a solo performance. **Up-retiree-hue** (Rapa Nui, Easter Islands) is to touch one's penis with the intention of masturbating, while the Japanese have several graphic terms for the experience. Male masturbation is referred to as **senzuri** (a thousand rubs), with the added refinement of **masu-kagami** (masturbating in front of a mirror). Female masturbation, by contrast, is described as **shiko shiko manzuri** (ten thousand rubs) and **suichi o ireru** (flicking the switch).

... and for many

Similar sensations can be experienced in company:

partousard (French) a participator in group sex

movimento (Italian) a circle of acquaintances who are actual or potential sexual partners

agapemone (Greek) an establishment where free love is practised

sacanagem (Brazilian Portuguese) the practice of openly seeking sexual pleasure with one or more partners other than one's primary partner (during Mardi Gras)

Pacific holiday

On the islands of Ulithi in the Western Pacific, the Micronesian people like to take a holiday from their regular lovemaking. **Pi supuhui** (literally, a hundred pettings) describes a holiday dedicated to mate-swapping. People pair up and go into the woods to share a picnic and make love. Married couples are not allowed to go together and the selection of new partners is encouraged. If there is an unequal number of participants, some couples may become threesomes.

The desired result or the result of desire

The French have a charming expression for this: **voir les anges**, which means to see angels.

Thumbs up

Gestures should be used carefully when abroad for fear of misunderstandings. The cheery thumbs-up used by the English or Americans means 'up yours' in the Middle East and 'sit on this' in Sardinia. In France, pressing a thumb against the fingertips means something is **ooh-la-la parfait** or just right, while in Egypt, the same gesture means 'stop right there'.

An American's sign for 'okay', made by touching the tip of the thumb to the tip of the forefinger, and used internationally by scuba divers, is an insult in Brazil. In some countries, the V sign can be negative, in others positive; in Italy, reversed, it approximates to 'to hell with you'. In some countries, flicking your thumb across the teeth tells the other person he's a cheapskate. Just about everywhere grabbing the crook of your elbow and raising your fist is rude. In the Arab world, the middle finger pointed downwards and moving up and down, with the palm horizontal, equates to a raised middle finger in England.

The Family Circle

bu yin, bu long, bu cheng gu
gong (*Chinese*)
unless one pretends to be stupid or deaf
it is difficult to be a mother-in-law or
father-in-law

Getting hitched

There comes a point, in most societies, where a relationship is formalized in law. As the Romanians say: **dragostea e oarbă, dar căsătoria îi găseşte leacul**, love is blind, but marriage finds a cure:

strga (Bulgarian) a survey or visit to the home of a prospective bride

kumoru aluweik (Khowar, Pakistan) to lure a girl into marriage

lobola (Manu Bantu, Zaire) the bride price (which is usually paid in cattle)

casarse de penalti (Spanish) to get married after discovering a pregnancy

dar el braguetazo (Spanish) the marriage of a poor man to a rich woman

skeinkjari (Faroese, Denmark) the man who goes among wedding guests offering them alcohol ('that popular chap')

Trouble and strife

Does one always live happily ever after? The evidence of our global languages suggests that it's not always the case:

desortijarse (Caribbean Spanish) to return the engagement ring

kotsuniku no araso (Japanese) domestic strife (literally, the fight between bones and flesh)

ava (Tahitian) wife (but it also means whisky)

pelotilla (Caribbean Spanish) argument among spouses

ainolektros (Ancient Greek) fatally wedded

talik (Malay) to marry with the stipulation of automatic divorce for a husband's desertion

rujuk (Indonesian) to remarry the wife you've already divorced

Yang

Sometimes, the man is clearly to blame when things go wrong (with the emphasis on infidelity, desertion and gambling):

pu'ukaula (Hawaiian) to set up one's wife as a stake in gambling

qum'us (Persian) one who pimps his own wife

talak (Arabic) a husband who frees himself from his wife

agunah (Hebrew) a woman whose husband has deserted her or has disappeared and who is restrained from remarrying until she shows a bill of divorce or proof of his death

bawusni (Persian) a wife whose husband does not love her and seldom visits

Yin

At other times the fault lies with the woman (with the emphasis on laziness, bullying and antipathy):

farik (Persian) a woman who hates her husband

jefa (Caribbean Spanish) a domineering wife

shiri ni shikareru (Japanese) a husband who is under his wife's thumb (literally, under her buttocks)

polohana'ole (Hawaiian) a woman who refuses to work but lives on her husband's earnings

baulero (Caribbean Spanish) a henpecked husband who cannot go out alone

purik (Indonesian) to return to one's parents' home as a protest against one's husband

Family matters

Once married, man and wife may find that their greatest problem is getting enough time alone. Extending the family can work both ways:

bol (Mayan, Mexico) foolish in-laws

sitike (Apache, USA) in-laws who are formally committed to help during crises

todamane (Tulu, India) entertaining a son-in-law or mother-in-law for the first time

bruja (Spanish, South America) a mother-in-law (literally, a witch)

biras (Malay) the relationship between two brothers' wives or two sisters' husbands

Chercher la femme?

When it comes to the family unit being threatened, why is there is no such thing as an **homme fatal**? Caribbean Spanish differentiates between a woman who prefers married men (**comadreja**, literally, a weasel) and one who lures them into extramarital relationships (**ciegamachos**). Can it really be that women are more predatory than men? Or is it that by luridly painting women as lustful (**aa'amo** in Hawaiian means 'an insatiable woman') and conniving (**alghunjar** is Persian for the feigned anger of a mistress), men the world over have cleverly avoided any blame for their own adulterous behaviour? Even when they're guilty, they try to keep the linguistic upper hand, if the German word **Drachenfutter** is anything to go by. Literally translated as 'dragon fodder' it describes the peace offerings that guilty husbands offer their spouses.

One cure for adultery

Rhaphanidosis was a punishment meted out to adulterous men by cuckolded husbands in Ancient Greece. It involved inserting a radish up their backside.

An avuncular solution

The Western ideal of a monogamous husband and wife is not universal. There is, for example, no word for father in Mosuo (China). The nearest translation for a male parental figure is **axia**, which means friend or lover; and while a child will have only one mother, he or she might have a sequence of **axia**. An **axia** has a series of nighttime trysts with a woman, after which he returns home to his mother. Any children resulting from these liaisons are raised in the woman's household. There are no fathers, husbands or marriages in Mosuo society. Brothers take care of their sisters' children and act as their fathers. Brothers and sisters live together all their lives in their mothers' homes.

Polygamy on ice

Other societies replace the complexities of monogamy with those of polygamy, as, for example, the Inuit of the Arctic:

angutawkun a man who exchanges wives with another man or one of the men who have at different times been married to the same woman

areodjarekput to exchange wives for a few days only, allowing a man sexual rights to his woman during that period

nuliinuaroak sharing the same woman; more specifically, the relationship between a man and his wife's lover when the husband has not consented to the arrangement

False friends

dad (Albanian) wet nurse or babysitter

babe (SiSwati, Swaziland) father or minister

mama (Georgian) father

brat (Russian) brother

parents (Portuguese) relatives

loo (Fulani, Mali) storage pot

bang (Albanian) paper bag

sin (Bosnian/Croatian/Serbian) son

Special relations

Whether it's because they have big families, time on their hands in large empty spaces, or for another reason, the Sami people of Northern Scandinavia have highly specific terms for family members and relationships: **goaski** are one's mother's elder sisters, and **sivjjot** is one's older sister's husband; one's mother's younger sisters are **muotta** and one's father's younger sisters are **siessa**; one's mother's brothers are **eanu** and her brothers' wives are **ipmi**; one's brother's wife is a **mangi**. The nearby Swedes exhibit a similar subtlety in their terms for grandfathers and grandmothers: **farfar** is a father's father, **morfar** is a mother's father, **farmor** is a father's mother and **mormor** is a mother's mother.

This pattern of precise names for individual family members had a parallel in an older society. Latin distinguished **patruus** (father's brother) from **avunculus** (mother's brother); and **matertera** (father's sister) from **amita** (mother's sister).

Of even earlier origins, the Australian Kamilaroi **nganuwaay** means a mother's cross-cousin's daughter and also a mother's father's sister's daughter as well as a mother's mother's brother's daughter's daughter as well as a mother's mother's brother's son's daughter.

Tahitian taio

Meanwhile, in the warm climate of Tahiti, the word **taio** (Maohi, French Polynesia) means a formal friendship between people not related by ancestors, which involves the sharing of everything, even sex partners. A **taio** relationship can be male-to-male, female-to-female or male-to-female.

Essential issue

Language testifies to the importance most cultures attach to having children, as well as the mixed emotions the little darlings bring with them. Yiddish, for example, details both extremes of the parental experience, **nakhes** being the mixture of pleasure and pride a parent gets from a child, and **tsuris** the grief and trouble:

izraf (Persian) producing ingenious, witty children

niyoga (Hindi) the practice of appointing a woman to bear a male heir who will be conceived by proxy

menguyel-uyel (Indonesian) to hug, cuddle and tickle someone (usually a child) as an expression of affection

gosh-pech (Persian) twisting the ears of a schoolboy as a punishment

abtar (Persian) one who has no offspring; a loser (literally, a bucket without a handle)

Parental ambitions

In contrast with the paternal indulgence of the French **fils à papa** (a son whose father makes things very easy for him) are some stricter maternal leanings:

kyoikumama (Japanese) a woman who crams her children to succeed educationally

ciegayernos (Caribbean Spanish) a woman who looks for a husband for her daughter

mammismo (Italian) maternal control and interference that continues into adulthood

Home is where the heart is

Not everyone lives in a standard box-like house:

berhane (Turkish) an impractically large mansion, rambling house

angase (Tulu, India) a building where the front part is used as a shop and the back as a residence

vidhvasram (Hindi) a home for widows

And rooms have many uses:

Folterkammer (German) a gym or exercise room (literally, a torture chamber)

ori (Khakas, Siberia) a hole in a yurt to store potatoes

tyconna (Anglo-Indian) an Indian basement room where the hottest part of the day is passed in the hottest season of the year

vomitarium (Latin) a room where a guest threw up in order to empty his stomach for more feasting

Bukumatala

In the Kiriwinian language of New Guinea a **bukumatala** is a 'young people's house', where adolescents go to stay on reaching puberty. As the main aim is to keep brothers and sisters away from the possibility of incestuous sexual contact close relatives will never stay in the same house. The boys return to the parental home for food and may help with the household work; the girls eat, work and occasionally sleep at home, but will generally spend the night with their adolescent sweethearts in one **bukumatala** or another.

Him b'long Missy Kween

An urgent need to communicate can create a language without native speakers. Pidgin, for example, has developed from English among people with their own native tongues. Fine examples of pidgin expressions in the Tok Pisin language of Papua New Guinea are: **liklik box you pull him he cry you push him he cry** (an accordion) and **bigfella iron walking stick him go bang along topside** (a rifle). When the Duke of Edinburgh visits Vanuatu, in the Pacific, he is addressed as **oldfella Pili-Pili him b'long Missy Kween**, while Prince Charles is **Pikinini b'long Kween**.

Clocking On

l'argent ne se trouve pas sous le sabot d'un cheval *(French)*
money isn't found under a horse's hoof

Tinker, tailor ...

The Japanese phrase for 'making a living' is **yo o wataru**, which literally means 'to walk across the world', and it's certainly true that when the chips are down there are some intriguing ways of earning a crust:

folapostes (Spanish) a worker who climbs telephone or electrical poles

geshtenjapjeks (Albanian) a street vendor of roast chestnuts

koshatnik (Russian) a dealer in stolen cats

dame-pipi (French) a female toilet assistant

tarriqu-zan (Persian) an officer who clears the road for a prince

kualanapuhi (Hawaiian) an officer who keeps the flies away from the sleeping king by waving a brush made of feathers

buz-baz (old Persian) a showman who made a goat and a monkey dance together

capoclaque (Italian) someone who coordinates a group of clappers

fyrassistent (Danish) an assistant lighthouse keeper

cigerci (Turkish) a seller of liver and lungs

lomilomi (Hawaiian) the masseur of the chief, whose duty it was to take care of his spittle and excrement

The daily grind

Attitudes to work vary not just from workplace to workplace, but from one side of the office to the other:

fucha (Polish) to use company time and resources for one's own purposes

haochi-lanzuo (Chinese) to be fond of food and averse to work

aviador (Spanish, Central America) a government employee who shows up only on payday

chupotero (Spanish) a person who works little but has several salaries

madogiwazoku (Japanese) those who have little to do (literally, window gazers)

jeito (Brazilian Portuguese) to find a way to get something done, no matter what the obstacles

Métro-boulot-dodo

This cheery French expression describes life in a none-too-optimistic way. Literally translated as 'tube-work-sleep' it summarizes the daily grind, hinting strongly that it's pointless.

Carrot ...

Motivation is a key factor, and employers who want maximum productivity find different ways of achieving this:

Mitbestimmung (German) the policy in industry of involving both workers and management in decision-making

vydvizhenchestvo (Russian) the system of promotion of workers to positions of responsibility and authority

kaizen (Japanese) the continuous improvement of working practices and personal efficiency as a business philosophy

... and stick

paukikape (Ancient Greek) the projecting collar worn by slaves while grinding corn in order to prevent them from eating it.

German work ethic

The Germans have long had a reputation for working hard. Inevitably, though, alongside the **Urlaubsmuffel**, or person who is against taking vacations, there is also the **Trittbrettfahrer** (literally, running-board rider), the person who profits from another's work. And along with the studious **Technonomade** (someone who conducts most of their business on the road, using laptops and mobiles), you will find the less scrupulous **schwarzarbeiten** (preferring to do work not reported for taxes).

False friends

biro (Arabic) office
adman (Arabic) offering better guaranty
ganga (Spanish) bargain
mixer (Hungarian) barman
slug (Gaulish) servant
fat (Cantonese) prosperity
hot (Romanian) thief
baker (Dutch) nurse

The deal

Others have less noble ways of getting ahead:

zhengquan-duoli (Chinese) to jockey for power and scramble
   for profit

jinetear el dinero (Spanish, Central America) to profit by
   delaying payment

tadlis (Persian) concealing the faults of goods on sale

qiang jingtou (Chinese) a fight by a cameraman for a vantage
   point (literally, stealing the show)

grilagem (Brazilian Portuguese) the old practice of putting a
   cricket in a box of newly faked documents, until the moving
   insect's excrement makes the papers look plausibly old and
   genuine (literally, cricketing)

On the take

If sharp practice doesn't work, then the best thing to do is cast all scruples aside:

bustarella (Italian) a cash bribe (literally, a little envelope)

dhurna (Anglo-Indian) extorting payment by sitting at the debtor's door and staying there without food, threatening violence until your demands are met

sola (Italian) a swindle in which you don't share the loot with your accomplice

sokaiya (Japanese) a blackmailer who has a few shares in a large number of companies and tries to extort money by threatening to cause trouble at the shareholders' annual general meetings

TST (Tahu Sama Tahu) (Indonesian) 'you know it, I know it': a verbal agreement between two people, one usually a government official, to cheat the state

Hard cash

In the end, it all comes down to one thing:

lechuga (Caribbean Spanish) a dollar bill (literally, lettuce)

kapusta (Russian) money (literally, cabbage)

mahiyana (Persian) monthly wages or fish jelly

wampum (Algonquian, Canada) strings of beads and polished shells, used as money by native Americans

Spongers

If you don't have much money yourself, there are always ways around the problem:

gorrero (Spanish, Central America) a person who always allows others to pay

piottaro (Italian) one who carries very little cash

Zechpreller (German) someone who leaves without paying the bill

dar mico (Caribbean Spanish) to consume without paying

seigneur-terrasse (French) one who spends much time but little money in a café (literally, a terrace lord)

Neither a borrower nor a lender be

Indonesian has the word **pembonceng** to describe someone who likes to use other people's facilities, but the Pascuense language of Easter Island has gone one step further in showing how the truly unscrupulous exploit friends and family. **Tingo** is to borrow things from a friend's house, one by one, until there's nothing left; while **hakamaroo** is to keep borrowed objects until the owner has to ask for them back.

What is yours is mine

It's a short step to outright crime:

mencomot (Indonesian) stealing things of small value such as food or drinks, partly for fun

baderotte (Danish) a beach thief

Agobilles (German) burglar's tools

ajane (Tulu, India) the noise of a thief

pukau (Malay) a charm used by burglars to make people fall asleep

azote de barrio (Spanish, Central America) a criminal who concentrates on a particular neighbourhood

accordéon (French) an extensive criminal record

A life of crime

Italian offers a rich vocabulary for different types of crime and criminal. **Smonta**, for example, is a theft carried out on a bus or train from which the perpetrator gets off as soon as possible, while **scavalco** (literally, climbing over) is a robbery carried out via a window or balcony. A night-time burglary is a **serenata** (literally, a serenade) which may well involve an **orchestra**, or gang of thieves, possibly accompanied by a **palo**, an accomplice who acts as lookout.

Extreme measures

If all else fails one of the following may be necessary:

nakkeskud (Danish) a shot in the back of the head
gusa (Japanese) to decapitate with a sword
rejam (Malay) to execute by pressing into mud

Hiding the evidence

Persian offers a refinement to the crude concept of 'murder'. The expression **war nam nihadan** means to kill and then bury someone, growing flowers over the grave in order to conceal it.

Chokey

As most career criminals would agree, the worst downside to a life of crime is getting caught:

kaush (Albanian) a prison cell or paper bag
squadretta (Italian) a group of prison guards who specialize in beating up inmates (literally, small squad)
fangfeng (Chinese) to let prisoners out for exercise or to relieve themselves
Kassiber (German) a letter smuggled out of jail; a secret coded message
jieyu (Chinese) to break into jail to rescue a prisoner
alba (Italian) the day one leaves prison after serving time

Executive essentials

Conclusions cannot always be drawn about historical connections. Some words are similar in numerous languages. Much linguistic research has led to the theory of an Ur-language (Indo–European) spoken some fifty thousand years ago, from which most other languages have descended. **Papa**, for example, is used for 'father' in seventy per cent of languages across the world.

Meanwhile, essential latterday vocabulary has crossed languages as easily as the jet-setting executive who uses it:

taxi is recognized in French, German, Swedish, Spanish, Danish, Norwegian, Dutch, Czech, Slovak, Portuguese, Hungarian and Romanian

sauna is recognized in Finnish, English, Portuguese, Spanish, Italian, French, German, Dutch, Danish, Lithuanian, Croatian/Bosnian/Serbian, Romanian and Norwegian

bank is recognized in Afrikaans, Amharic (Ethiopia), Bengali, Creole, Danish, Dutch, Frisian (Germany and Holland), German, Gujarati (India), Hungarian, Indonesian, Malay, Norwegian, Polish, Sinhala (Sri Lanka), Swedish and Wolof (Senegal and Gambia)

hotel is recognized in Afrikaans, Amharic, Asturian (Spain), Bulgarian, Catalan, Croatian/Bosnian/Serbian, Czech, Danish, Dutch, Frisian (Germany and Holland), Galician (Spain), German, Icelandic, Polish, Portuguese, Romanian, Slovak, Slovenian, Tswana (Botswana), Ukrainian and Yiddish

Time Off

il giocare non è male, ma è male
il perdere *(Italian)*
there is no harm in playing but great harm
in losing

Fun and games

Since the start of time the desire to fill it has resulted in a wide range of recreations. Simplest are the games played by children the world over:

toto (Cook Islands Maori) a shout given in a game of hide-and-seek to show readiness for the search to begin

pokku (Tulu, India) the throwing of pebbles up in the air and catching them as they fall

kabaddi (Pakistan) a game where players take it in turn to hold their breath

bakpi (Ulwa, Nicaragua) a game in which one is swung round in circles until dizzy

cnapan (Welsh) a game where each side tries to drive a wooden ball as far as possible in one direction

kula'i wawae (Hawaiian) the pushing of one's feet against others while seated

kaengurustylte (Danish) a pogo stick (literally, kangaroo stilt)

Frozen walrus carcass

There are games that are highly specific to their culture and environment, such as the Inuit **igunaujannguaq**, which literally means frozen walrus carcass. This is a game where the person in the centre tries to remain stiff and is held in place by the feet of the people who are sitting in a circle. He is passed around the ring, hand over hand. Whoever drops him is the next 'frozen walrus carcass'.

Honing your skills

As we grow up, what we look for in a game becomes increasingly challenging:

shash-andaz (Persian) someone who tries to juggle with six balls so that four are always in the air

antyaksari (Hindi) a pastime in which participants recite verses in turn, the first word of each new verse being the same as the last of the preceding one

kipapa (Hawaiian) to balance on top of a surfboard

waterponie (Afrikaans) a jet ski

elastikspring (Danish) bungee jumping

The beautiful game

One game in particular has achieved international pre-eminence, and a range of closely observed terms to describe it:

armario (Spanish) an awkward or unskilled player (literally, a wardrobe)

wayra jayt'a (Quechuan, Peru) a poor player (literally, an air kicker)

cazar (Spanish) to kick one's opponent and not the ball

ariete (Spanish) a battering ram (centre forward)

verkac (Turkish) passing and running

baile, danze (Spanish) and **melina** (Italian) two players on the same team kicking the ball back and forth to kill time

roligan (Danish) a non-violent supporter

Taking a punt

Sometimes, fun is not enough; chance or expertise has to be made more exciting by speculation:

yetu (Tulu, India) gambling in which a coin is tossed and a bet laid as to which side it will fall on

quiniela (Spanish, USA) a form of betting in which the punter must choose the first and second-place winners in a race, though not necessarily in the correct order

parani (Cook Islands Maori) to put up a stake at poker without examining one's cards

The moral perhaps being that it's better to be the Persian **kuz-baz**, one who lends money to gamblers, than a **mukhtir**, one who risks his property in gambling.

Fingers crossed

Some people are born **lechero**, a Latin American Spanish word for lucky, literally meaning a milkman. Others may be less fortunate:

smolař (Czech) a person dogged by bad luck

apes (Indonesian) to have double bad luck

kualat (Indonesian) to be bound to have bad luck as a result of behaving badly

Break a leg

It's intriguing that wishing people good luck often takes the form of willing ill fortune on them. The German **Hals und Beinbruch**, for example, takes the spirit of the English expression 'break a leg' and goes one step further – it translates as 'break your neck and a leg'. The Italians offer an even more gruesome prospect: the cheery wish **in bocca al lupo** means 'into the mouth of the wolf'.

The competitive streak

Everyone likes to win, but the methods employed to get ahead range from the inventive to the underhand:

chupar rueda (Spanish) running or cycling behind another to benefit from reduced wind resistance (literally, to suck wheel)

kunodesme (Ancient Greek) tying a string round the foreskin to stop the penis getting in the way during athletics (literally, putting the dog on a lead)

sirind (Persian) entangling legs in wrestling to trip your opponent (also a noose for catching prey by the foot)

poki (Cook Islands Maori) to deal cards from the bottom of the pack (i.e. unfairly)

False friends

boghandel (Danish) bookshop

rain (Arabic) viewer, spectator

arse (Turkish) violin bow

jerk (French) praise for an accomplished dancer

pensel (Swedish) paintbrush

catch (French) all-in wrestling

Crooning

For those without sporting interest or prowess, entertainment can be found in the realms of music . . .

iorram (Scottish Gaelic) a rowing song

dizlanmak (Turkish) to keep humming to yourself

Ohrwurm (German) a catchy tune that gets stuck in the brain or rapidly obsesses an entire population (literally, an ear worm)

ngak-ngik-ngok (Indonesian) a derogatory reference to the popularity of rock music in the 1960s (which was much despised by the late President Sukarno)

Twirling

. . . or of dancing

raspar canillas (Spanish, Central America) to dance (literally, to scrape shins)

zapateado (Spanish) the fast footwork and stamping feet used in dancing

mbuki-mvuki (Bantu, Zaire) to take off one's clothes in order to dance

Ball paradox (German) a ball at which women ask men to dance

verbunkos (Hungarian) a dance performed to persuade people to enlist in the army

Clubbing

The Italians helpfully differentiate between the staff outside and inside a night club: the **buttadentro**, the one who throws you in, is the person in charge of choosing who gets through the door; while the **buttafuori**, the one who throws you out, is the bouncer.

Channel surfing

For those who prefer to stay at home, there's always the television, or **Pantoffelkino** (slippers cinema), as it's described in German. The Romani language of the Gypsies takes a rather sterner view, regarding it as a **dinnilos-dicking-muktar**, or fool's looking-box. Those with extra channels seem to be viewed as a cut-above in France, where **cablé** has now acquired the secondary sense of 'hip and trendy'.

Hi-tech

Having invented numerous machines to give us free time, we now struggle to come up with others to help fill it:

tamagotchi (Japanese) a lovable egg (an electronic device which copies the demands for food or attention of a pet)

khali khukweni (Zulu) a mobile phone (literally, to make a noise in the pocket)

dingdong (Indonesian) computer games in an arcade

toelva (Icelandic) a computer (formed from the words for digit and prophetess)

xiaoxia (Chinese) small lobsters (new internet users)

The arts

There are some pastimes that are elevated, by their practitioners and admirers, onto an altogether higher plane:

sprezzatura (Italian) the effortless technique of a great artist

wabi (Japanese) a flawed detail that enhances the elegance of the whole work of art

ostranenie (Russian) the process by which art makes familiar perceptions seem strange

Verfremdungseffekt (German) a dramatic technique that encourages the audience to preserve a sense of critical detachment from a play (literally, an alienating effect)

Philistines

Those who aren't impressed by artistic claims have coined a different vocabulary:

megillah (Yiddish) an unnecessarily long and tiresome story or letter

de pacotilla (Spanish) a third-rate writer or actor

Rolling up

In our health-conscious world, can smoking still be regarded as recreation?

segatura (Italian) a cigarette made by mixing cigarette butts (literally, sawdust)

bakwe (Kapampangan, Philippines) to smoke a cigarette with the lit end in the mouth

nakurit'sya (Russian) to smoke to one's heart's content

zakurit'sya (Russian) to make oneself ill by excessive smoking

Married in a brothel

Some words must remain a mystery to all except native speakers. You would have had to have lived in these places for quite a while to understand how to use correctly some of the following, which in their simply translated definitions contain what seem to us contradictory meanings:

hay kulu (Zarma, Nigeria) anything, nothing and also everything

irpadake (Tulu, India) ripe and unripe

sitoshna (Tulu, India) cold and hot

merripen (Romani, Gypsy) life and death

gift (Norwegian) poison and married

magazinshchik (Russian) a shopkeeper and a shoplifter

danh t (Vietnamese) a church and a brothel

aloha (Hawaiian) hello and goodbye (the word has many other meanings including love, compassion, welcome and good wishes)

Eating and Drinking

olcsó húsnak híg a leve *(Hungarian)*
cheap meat produces thin gravy

Hunting, shooting . . .

In many parts of the world putting together a meal isn't always simply a matter of making a quick trip to the local supermarket:

ortektes (Khakas, Siberia) to hunt together for ducks

geragai (Malay) a hook for catching crocodiles

sumpit (Malay) to shoot with a blowpipe

tu'utu'u (Rapa Nui, Easter Island) to hit the mark time and again (shooting with arrows)

ajawy (Wayampi, Brazil) to hit the wrong target

. . . and fishing

Fishing can be equally labour-intensive:

ta'iti (Cook Islands Maori) to catch fish by encircling a rock with a net and frightening them out

kapau'u (Hawaiian) to drive fish into a waiting net by splashing or striking the water with a leafy branch

lihnaka inska wauhwaia (Ulwa, Nicaragua) to slap the water and cause the fish to jump into a boat

nono (Rapa Nui, Easter Island) fish thrown onto the beach by the waves or which jump out of the water into a boat

kusyad (Persian) hard black stone thrown into the water to attract fish

fiskevaer (Norwegian) good weather for fishing

ah chamseyah chay (Chorti, Guatemala) someone who fishes with dynamite

pau heoheo (Hawaiian) a person who returns from fishing without any fish

Global gastronomy

When it comes to the extraordinary things that people around the world enjoy putting in their mouths, it's certainly true that one man's meat is another man's poison:

ptsha (Yiddish) cow's feet in jelly

poronkieli (Finnish) reindeer tongue

kokorec (Turkish) roasted sheep's intestines

nama-uni (Japanese) raw sea urchin

Beuschel (German) stewed calves' lungs

acitron (Mexican Spanish) candied cactus

somad (Sherpa, Nepal) cheese that is old and smelly

calimocho (Spanish) a combination of Coca-Cola and red wine

Gummiadler (German) tough roast chicken (literally, rubber eagle)

marilopotes (Ancient Greek) a gulper of coal dust

ampo (Malay) edible earth

Menu envy

In some cases, though, it's the unfamiliar word rather than the food itself that may alarm the outsider:

flab (Gaelic) a mushroom
moron (Welsh) a carrot
aardappel (Dutch) a potato (literally, earth apple)
bikini (Spanish) a toasted ham and cheese sandwich
gureepufuruutsu (Japanese) a grapefruit

Can't cook ...

We all know the benefits of **lumur** (Malay), smearing ingredients with fat during cooking. But even that doesn't always prevent **kanzo** (Hausa, Nigeria), burnt food stuck to the bottom of the pot. Perhaps it would help to know the right moment for **nisar-qararat** (Persian), cold water poured into a pot to stop it getting burnt. The only fail-safe way of escaping this is to buy your food **boli boli** (Aukan, Suriname) – already cooked.

Bon appetit

Now we're ready to eat . . .

protintheuo (Ancient Greek) to pick out the dainty bits beforehand, to help oneself first

muka (Hawaiian) a smacking sound with the lips, indicating that the food is tasty

pakupaku (Japanese) to eat in big mouthfuls or take quick bites

parmaklamak (Turkish) to eat with one's fingers

sikkiwok (Inuit) to drink with your chin in the water

nusarat (Persian) crumbs falling from a table which are picked up and eaten as an act of piety

Boring food

The Japanese are emphatic about how dull food can be: **suna o kamu yo na** means 'like chewing sand'. They even have an evocative term for rehashed food: **nibansenji**, meaning 'brewing tea for the second time using the same tea-leaves'.

Cupboard love

Those who have food on the table will always be popular:

giomlaireachd (Scottish Gaelic) the habit of dropping in at meal times

aimerpok (Inuit) to visit expecting to receive food

luqma-shumar (Persian) one who attends feasts uninvited and counts the number of mouthfuls

Snap, crackle, pop!

Is it the way they hear it? Or is it simply what sells the product? The sound of Rice Crispies crackling and popping is very different across Europe:

French: **Cric! Crac! Croc!**
German: **Knisper! Knasper! Knusper!**
Spanish: **Cris! Cras! Cros!**

Rice

In Japan, **gohan** (literally, honourable food) comes in a bowl and means rice that is ready for eating. But it's also a general name for rice and even extends in meaning to 'meal'. At the other end of the spectrum is **okoge**, which is the scorched rice stuck on the bottom of the pan.

False friends

prune (French) plum
gin (Phrygian, Turkey) to dry out
korn (Swedish) barley
sik (Ukrainian) juice
glass (Swedish) ice cream
prick (Thai) pepper
chew (Amharic, Ethiopia) salt

Hawaiian bananas

Hawaii's traditional cuisine is based on quite a restricted list of ingredients: fish (there are 65 words alone for describing fishing nets), sweet potato (108 words), sugarcane (42) and bananas (47). The following are among the most descriptive words for this fruit:

mai'a kaua lau a banana, dark green when young, and yellow and waxy when mature

kapule a banana hanging until its skin has black spots

palaku a thoroughly ripe banana

maui to wring the stem of a bunch of bananas to cause it to ripen

pola the hanging down of the blossom of a banana palm or a bunch of bananas

halane a large bunch of bananas

hua'alua a double bunch of bananas

manila a banana tree not used for fruit but for rope fibre

lele a tall wild banana placed near the altar, offered to the gods and also used for love magic

Replete

As the meal enters its final stages, a sense of well-being descends on the diner – unless, of course, you're suffering from **bersat** (Malay), food that has gone down the wrong way . . .

uitbuiken (Dutch) to take your time at dinner, relaxing between courses (literally, the expansion of the stomach)

nakkele (Tulu, India) a man who licks whatever the food has been served on

slappare (Italian) to eat everything, even to the point of licking the plate

'akapu'aki'aki (Cook Islands Maori) to belch repeatedly

Post-prandial

After it's all over, what are you left with?

femlans (Ullans, Northern Ireland) the remains of a meal

sunasorpok (Inuit) to eat the remains of others' food

shitta (Persian) food left at night and eaten in the morning

Food poisoning

Visitors to Easter Island would be advised to distinguish between the Rapa Nui words **hakahana** (leaving cooked food for another day) and **kai hakahana** (food from the previous day that is starting to rot).

Hunger

Food cannot always be taken for granted. **Homowo** is a Ghanaian word that means 'hooting at hunger'. Local oral tradition recalls a distant past when the rains failed and there was a terrible famine on the Accra Plains, the home of the Ga people. When a good harvest finally came and there was more than enough to eat once again, the Ghanaians celebrated by holding a festival, still celebrated to this day, that ridiculed hunger.

Daily Bread

Food often figures in colloquial sayings and proverbs, as this selection from Spain shows:

quien con hambre se acuesta con pan suena whoever goes to bed hungry dreams of bread (to have a bee in one's bonnet)

agua fría y pan caliente, nunca hicieron buen vientre cold water and hot bread never made a good belly (oil and water never mix)

pan tierno y leña verde, la casa pierde fresh bread and green firewood lose the house (two wrongs do not make a right)

vale bolillo it's worth a piece of bread (it doesn't matter)

con su pan se lo coma may he eat it with bread (good luck to him)

Quenched

After all this talk of food and eating, it's hard not to feel thirsty:

gurfa (Arabic) the amount of water scooped up in one hand
tegok (Malay) the water one can swallow at a gulp
qamus (Persian) [a well] so abundant in water that the bucket disappears
yewh-ma (Wagiman, Australia) to scrape out a hole in the sand to collect fresh water
jabh (Persian) arriving at a well and finding no water

Bakbuk bakbuk bakbuk

Like the English expression 'glug glug glug', the Hebrew word for bottle, **bakbuk**, derives from the sound of liquid being poured from it.

Pythons and sponges

Those who have not experienced **sgriob** (Scottish Gaelic), the itchiness that overcomes the upper lip just before taking a sip of whisky, may have suffered from **olfrygt** (Viking Danish), the fear of a lack of ale. And it's not always a fish the world drinks like:

beber como uma esponja (Portuguese) to drink like a sponge
uwabami no yo ni nomu (Japanese) to drink like a python
geiin suru (Japanese) to drink like a whale
bjor-reifr (Old Icelandic) cheerful from beer-drinking
sternhagelvoll (German) completely drunk (literally, full of stars and hail)

Plastered

To the sober, it's always intriguing to see what drunken people are convinced they can do when under the influence, such as trying to walk in a straight line (**kanale'o** in Hawaiian). Perhaps it's best to bear in mind the Romanian proverb **dacă doi spun că eşti beat, du-te şi te culcă**, if two people say you're drunk, go to sleep.

The morning after

at have tømmermaend (Danish) having a hangover (literally, to have carpenters, i.e. hearing the noise of drilling, sawing, etc.)

Katzenjammer (German) a very severe hangover (literally, the noise made by extremely miserable cats)

A useful excuse

As they say in Aymara (Bolivia and Peru), **umjayanipxitütuwa** – they must have made me drink.

Doormat dandy

Languages are full of traps for the unwary, particularly when it comes to words that sound similar but mean very different things:

Spanish: **el papa** the Pope; **la papa** potato
Albanian: **cubar** ladies' man, womanizer; **cube** proud, courageous girl
Kerja, Indonesia: **aderana** prostitute; **aderòna** perfume
Italian: **zerbino** doormat; **zerbinotto** dandy
Arabic: **khadij** premature child; **khidaj** abortion
Albanian: **shoq** husband; **shog** bald man; **shop** blockhead

Below Par

u miericu pietusu fa la piaga
verminusa (*Calabrian, Italy*)
*the physician with too much pity will cause
the wound to fester*

Ouch!

The exclamation denoting pain has many varieties. If you touch a boiling kettle in Korea you cry **aiya**, in the Philippines **aruy** and in France **aïe**. In Russian you scream **oj**, in Danish **uh** and in German **aua**.

Atishoo!

In Japan one sneeze signifies praise (**ichi home**); two sneezes, criticism (**ni-kusashi**); three sneezes, disparagement (**san-kenashi**),

while four or more sneezes are taken to mean, quite reasonably, that a cold is on its way (**yottsu-ijo wa kaze no moto**). Meanwhile, in Mexico, one sneeze is answered with the word **salud** (health); two sneezes with **dinero** (money); three sneezes with **amor** (love); four or more sneezes with **alergías** (allergies); laughter often accompanies four sneezes, because health, money and love are obviously more desirable than allergies.

Bless you!

In response to someone sneezing, the Germans say **Gesundheit**, 'health to you', and the French **à tes souhaits**, literally, 'to your wishes'. In Sierre Leone, Mende speakers say **biseh**, or 'thank you'; in Malagasy, the language of Madagascar, they say **velona**, 'alive', while the Bembe speakers of the Congo say **kuma**, 'be well'. In Tonga a sneeze is often taken to be a sign that your loved one is missing you.

Sneezing protocol

In Brazil, they say **saúde** (health) and the sneezer answers **amen**. In Arabic, the sneezer says **alhumdullilah** ('praise be to God') first, to which the other person responds **yarhamukumu Allah** ('may God have mercy on you'). The sneezer then replies to that with **athabakumu Allah** ('may God reward you'). In Iran, things are more complex. There they say **afiyat bashe** ('I wish you good health') and the sneezer replies **elahi shokr** ('thank God for my health'). After the first sneeze Iranians are then supposed to stop whatever they were doing for a few minutes before continuing. If the sneeze interrupts a decision it is taken as an indication not to go ahead. Ignoring the single sneeze means risking bad luck. However, a second sneeze clears the slate.

Falling ill

The miseries of the sick bed are universally known:

smertensleje (Danish) to toss and turn on your bed in pain

fanbing (Chinese) to have an attack of one's old illness

ruttlin (Cornish) the sound of phlegm rattling in the bronchial tubes

miryachit (Russian) a disease in which the sufferer mimics everything that is said or done by another

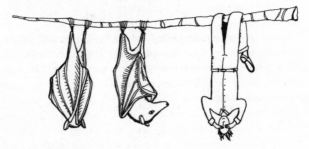

False friends

gem (Mongolian) defect

lavman (Turkish) enema

angel (Dutch) sting

bad (Arabic) amputation

bladder (Dutch) blister

santa (Egyptian Arabic) wart

turd (Persian) delicate or fragile

Bedside manner

Illness demands sympathy, but the Indonesian word **besuk** suggests that this is not always forthcoming. It means to refuse to visit a sick person. Possibly with good reason:

bawwal (Persian) one who pisses in bed
osurgan (Turkish) someone who farts a lot
dobol (Indonesian) to have a swollen anus
ra'ora'oa (Cook Islands Maori) to have swollen testicles
kepuyuh (Indonesian) to have to urinate
jerrkjerrk (Wagiman, Australia) diarrhoea
chiasse (French) runs induced by fear

Impatient?

Perhaps the most telling word in the lexicon of sickness is the Chinese word **huiji-jiyi** – to avoid following your doctor's advice for fear of being recognized as the sufferer of a disease.

Vowelless

The Tashlhiyt dialect of Berber (North Africa) is known for its vowelless words: **tzgr**, she crossed, and **rglx**, I locked. Among the longest are **tkkststt**, you took it off, and **tftktstt**, you sprained it. And if we accept 'r' as a consonant (which is debatable in Czech, as 'l' and 'r' function as sonorants and so fulfil the role of a vowel) then words consisting entirely of consonants are common in their language: **krk**, neck; **prst**, finger or toe; **smrk**, pine tree; **smrt**, death. Words beginning with five consonants are not unknown: **ctvrt**, quarter and **ctvrtek**, Thursday. Likewise in Croatian/Bosnian/Serbian there are: **crkva**, church; **mrkva**, carrot; **trg**, market and **zrtva**, vinegar.

From Cradle to Grave

xian zhang de meimao, bi bu shang
hou zhang de huzi *(Chinese)*
*the eyebrows that started growing first can't
compare with the beard that started growing
later*

In the family way

Pregnancy can be something of a mixed blessing:

mirkha (Quechuan, Peru) the freckles or spots on a woman's
face during pregnancy

waham (Arabic) the craving for certain foods during pregnancy

tafarrus (Persian) the fainting of a pregnant woman

Birth pains

When it comes to childbirth, English tends to be coy. There is no English equivalent for the Inuit word **paggiq**, which describes the flesh torn as a woman delivers a baby, nor for the Japanese **chigo-bami** – bites inflicted on a mother's nipple by a suckling baby. As for the less painful aspects of giving birth, we lack the Indonesian word **uek**, the sound of a baby crying when being born, the very precise Ulwa word from Nicaragua, **asahnaka**, to hold a child on one's hip with its legs straddling the hipbone facing the mother's side, let alone the Persian term **kundamoya**, which is the hair a child is born with.

Birthing partner

The Inuit have a word **tunumiaq** which denotes the person who supports a pregnant woman's back during labour.

First steps in the deep Pacific

In Rapa Nui (Easter Island) there are five detailed words to describe a baby's early progress: **kaukau** is a newborn baby first moving its hands and feet; **puepue** is when it begins to distinguish people and objects; **tahuri** is when it starts to move from side to side; **totoro** is when it's learned to crawl; **mahaga** is when it is able to stand by itself.

Toddling

English is strangely deficient when it comes to observing the many stages of development:

teete (Zarma, Nigeria) to teach a toddler how to walk

menetah (Indonesian) to help a little child walk by holding its hands to keep it in balance

pokankuni (Tulu, India) to learn by looking at others

keke (Hawaiian) a word of caution to children to cover their nakedness

Growing pains

The next few years are crucial:

polekayi (Tulu, India) writing in a large crooked hand as children tend to do

qiangda (Chinese) a race to be the first to answer a question

nylentik (Indonesian) to hit a child's ear with the index finger

paski (Tulu, India) punishing a boy by making him alternate between standing and sitting with his arms crossed and both ears seized by his fingers

zhangjin (Chinese) the progress made in one's intellectual or moral education

Polterabend (German) a stag party for both sexes at which crockery is broken celebrating the end of their single lives

ronin (Japanese) a student who has failed a university entrance examination and is waiting to retake it (adapted from its original sense of a lordless wandering samurai warrior)

Boys and girls

Some cultures go further than merely differentiating between children and adolescents. The Indonesian word **balita** refers to those under five years old; the Hindi term **kumari** means a girl between ten and twelve, while **bala** is a young woman under the age of sixteen. The Cook Islands Maoris continue the sequence with **mapu**, a youth from about sixteen to twenty-five.

False friends

compromisso (Portuguese) engagement
embarazada (Spanish) pregnant
anus (Latin) old woman
chin (Persian) one who catches money thrown at
   weddings
moon (Khakas, Siberia) to hang oneself
bath (Scottish Gaelic) to drown
hoho (Hausa, Nigeria) condolences

Mid-life crisis

Before we know it, the carefree days of our youth are just fading memories:

sanada arba' (Arabic) to be pushing forty
parebos (Ancient Greek) being past one's prime
kahala (Arabic) to be an old fogey at the height of one's life
Torschlusspanik (German) the fear of diminishing
    opportunities as one gets older (literally, gate-closing panic);
    this word is often applied to women worried about being too
    old to have children

Getting older Hawaiian-style

The Hawaiians have a highly specific vocabulary to describe the effects of what the Germans call **Lebensabend**, the twilight of life:

'aua a woman beginning to become wrinkled
ku'olo an old man with sagging cheeks
kani ko'o an aged man who needs to carry a cane
kani mo'opuna the state of old age when one has many
    grandchildren
hakalunu extreme old age, as when one is no longer able to
    walk
ka'i koko bedridden; so old one needs to be carried in a net
pala lau hala the advanced loss of hair; the last stage of life

Kicking the bucket

Other languages have highly inventive euphemisms for the tricky subject of passing on:

nolikt karoti (Latvian) to put down the spoon

colgar los guantes (Spanish, Central America) to hang up the gloves

het hoek omgaan (Dutch) to go around the corner

bater a bota/esticar a perna (Portuguese) to hit the boot or to stretch the leg

avaler son bulletin de naissance (French) to swallow one's birth certificate

The final reckoning

adjal (Indonesian) the predestined hour of one's death

Liebestod (German) dying for love or because of a romantic tragedy

pagezuar (Albanian) the state of dying before enjoying the happiness that comes with being married or seeing one's children married

Chinese whispers

Chinese has a rich vocabulary when it comes to the last moments of life:

huiguang fanzhao the momentary recovery of someone who is dying

yiyan a person's last words

yiyuan a person's last or unfulfilled wish

mingmu to die with one's eyes closed, to die without regret

txiv xaiv a funeral singer whose songs bring helpful, didactic messages from the dead person to the survivors

Last rites

In the end the inevitable takes its course:

talkin (Indonesian) to whisper to the dying (i.e. words read at the end of a funeral to remind the dead person of what to say to the angels of death)

farjam-gah (Persian) the final home (grave)

tunillattukkuuq (Inuit) the act of eating at a cemetery

akika (Swahili) a domestic feast held either for a child's first haircut or for its burial

The long of it

Among languages that build up very long words for both simple and complex concepts are those defined as 'polysynthetic', and many of them are found in Australia or Papua New Guinea. The Aboriginal Mayali tongue of Western Arnhem Land is an example, forming highly complex verbs able to express a complete sentence, such as: **ngabanmarneyawoyhwarrgahganjginjeng**, meaning 'I cooked the wrong meat for them again'. (This breaks down into **nga**: I, **ban**: them, **marne**: for, **yawoyh**: again, **warrgah**: wrongly directed action, **ganj**: meat, **ginje**: cook, **ng**: past tense.) In the Australian language known as Western Desert, **palyamunurringkutjamunurtu** means 'he or she definitely did not become bad'.

Germans are not the only ones who like to create complex compound words as nouns. **Arbejdsløsheds-understøttelse** is Danish for unemployment benefit, while **tilpasningsvanskeligheder** means 'adjustment difficulties'. **Precipitevolissimevolmente** is Italian for 'as fast as possible'. And in the Tupi-Guarani Apiaká language of Brazil, **tapa-há-ho-huegeuvá** means rubber.

But maybe the laurels should go to the Ancient Greek playwright Aristophanes who devised the word **lopado-temacho-selacho-galeo-kranio-leipsano-drim-hu-potrimmato-silphio-karabo-melito-katakechumeno-kichl-epikossuphophatto-perister-alektruon-opto-kephallio-kigklo-peleio-lagoio-siraio-baphe-tragano-pterugon**, a dish compounded of all kinds of dainties, fish, fowl and sauces.

Otherworldly

zig then ma che; dam choe ma ha
(Dzongkha, Bhutan)
do not start your worldly life too late; do not start your religious life too early

Beyond the veil

So what lies beyond the beauties of life, in sight, sound and smell? Do we live for ever? And if so, can any of us ever return?

iwang wayaka (Ulwa, Nicaragua) a spirit that comes out after a
   person dies, makes noises and yet is never seen
tarniqsuqtuq (Inuit) a communication with a spirit that is
   unable to ascend
raskh (Persian) the transmigration of the human soul into a
   plant or tree

hrendi thenok (Sherpa, Nepal) to get in touch with the soul of
   a dead person
bodach (Scottish Gaelic) the ghost of an old man that comes
   down the chimney to terrorize children who have been
   naughty

Spooked in Sumatra

The Indonesians have a particularly varied vocabulary to describe the inhabitants of the spirit world and their attempts to menace the living:

wewe an ugly female ghost with drooping breasts

keblak a ghost cockerel which frightens people at night with the sound of its flapping wings

kuntilanak a ghost masquerading as a beautiful woman to seduce men who are then horrified to find that she actually has a large hole in her back

Looking into the future

A cynical old Chinese proverb offers the thought **ruo xin bu, maile wu; mai gua kou, mei liang dou**: 'if you believe in divination you will end up selling your house to pay the diviners'. But attempting to see into the future has been a constant in all societies for thousands of years:

aayyaf (Arabic) predicting the future by observing the flight of birds

ustukhwan-tarashi (Persian) divination using the shoulder-blade of a sheep

haruspex (Latin) a priest who practised divination by examining the entrails of animals

kilo lani (Hawaiian) an augury who can read the clouds

sortes (Latin) the seeking of guidance by the chance selection of a passage in a book

mandal (Arabic) prophesying while staring into a mirror-like surface

Hide away

Scottish Highlanders formerly had an unusual way of divining the future, known as **taghairm**. This involved wrapping a man in the hide of a freshly butchered bullock and leaving him alone by a waterfall, under a cliff-face, or in some other wild and deserted place. Here he would think about his problem; and whatever answer he came up with was supposed to have been given to him by the spirits who dwelt in such forbidding spots.

False friends

monaco (Italian) monk
fish (Arabic) Easter, Passover
alone (Italian) halo
fall (Breton) bad
lav (Armenian) good
bog (Russian) god

God willing

The French have a term, **bondieuserie**, which means ostentatious piety. But for many the solace of prayer and faith is both necessary and private:

saruz-ram (Persian) the first light breaking upon one committed to a contemplative life

rasf (Persian) the joining together of the feet in prayer (also the joining of stones in pavements)

thondrol (Dzongkha, Bhutan) the removal of sins through the contemplation of a large religious picture

kuoha (Hawaiian) a prayer used to bring a wife to love her husband and a husband to love his wife

tekbir (Arabic) to proclaim the greatness of God, by repeating **allahu akkbar**, 'Allah is great'

pasrah (Indonesian) to leave a problem to God

The short of it

Among single letter words to be found among the world's languages are the following:

u (Samoan) an enlarged land snail
u (Xeta, Brazil) to eat animal meat
u (Burmese) a male over forty-five (literally, uncle)
i (Korean) a tooth
m (Yakut, Siberia) a bear; an ancestral spirit

All Creatures Great and Small

meglio è esser capo di lucertola
che coda di dragone *(Italian)*
*better be the head of a lizard than the tail
of a dragon*

Animal crackers

'Every dog has his day'; 'you can take a horse to water, but you can't make it drink'; 'a cat may look at a king'. Animals crop up left, right and centre in English sayings and phrases, and in those of other languages too:

leben wie die Made im Speck (German) to live like a maggot in bacon (life of Riley)

van een kale kip kan je geen veren plukken (Dutch) you can't pluck feathers from a bald hen (get blood out of a stone)

olla ketunhäntä kainalossa (Finnish) to have a foxtail under your armpits (ulterior motives)

estar durmiendo con la mona (Spanish) to be sleeping with the monkey (be drunk)

eine Kröte schlucken (German) to swallow a toad (make a concession grudgingly)

bhains ke age bansuri bajana (Hindi) to play a flute in front of a buffalo (cast pearls before swine)

vot gde sobaka zaryta (Russian) that's where the dog is buried (the crux of the matter)

avaler des couleuvres (French) to swallow grass snakes (endure humiliation)

karincalanmak (Turkish) to be crawling with ants (have pins and needles)

Dragon's head

The Japanese are particularly fond of animal metaphors:

itachigokko weasels' play (a vicious circle)

gyuho an ox's walk (a snail's pace)

neko no hitai a cat's forehead (a very small area)

yabuhebi ni naru to poke at a bush and get a snake (to backfire)

ryuto dabi ni owaru to start with a dragon's head and end with a snake's tail (to peter out)

dasoku snake legs (excessive or superfluous)

tora ni naru to become a tiger (to get roaring drunk)

unagi no nedoko an eel's bed (a long narrow place)

mushi no idokoro ga warui the location of the worm is bad (in a bad mood)

kirinji a giraffe child (prodigy)

kumo no ko o chirasu yo ni like scattering baby spiders (in all directions)

inu to saru a dog and a monkey (to be on bad terms)

Ships of the desert

As you might expect, the more important an animal is to a particular culture, the more words there are for it. The cattle-herding Masai of Kenya and Tanzania, for example, have seventeen distinct words for cattle; the jungle-based Baniwa tribe of Brazil has twenty-nine for ant (with a range that includes the edible); while in Somali there are no fewer than forty-three words relating to camels of every possible variety. Here are a few:

qoorqab an uncastrated male camel

awradhale a stud camel that always breeds male camels

gurgurshaa a docile pack-camel suitable for carrying delicate items

sidig one of two female camels suckling the same baby camel

guran a herd of camels no longer producing milk that is kept away from dwelling areas

baatir a mature female camel that has had no offspring

gulguuluc the low bellow of a camel when it is sick or thirsty

cayuun camel spit

u maqaarsaar to put the skin of a dead baby camel on top of a living one in order to induce its mother to give milk

uusmiiro to extract drinking water from the stomach of a camel to drink during a period of drought

guree to make room for a person to sit on a loaded camel

tulud one's one and only camel

Persian also has its own detailed camel vocabulary that suggests an even more recalcitrant beast:

nakhur a camel that will not give milk until her nostrils are tickled

wakhd a camel that throws out its feet in the manner of an
   ostrich
munqamih a camel that raises its head and refuses to drink
   any more
zirad a rope tied round a camel's neck to prevent it from
   vomiting on its rider

Horses for courses

Many languages have very specific words to describe not only types
of horse but also its activities and attributes. In the Quechuan language of Peru, **tharmiy** is a horse that stands on its hind legs and
kicks out with its forelegs. The Bulgar **lungur** is an unfit horse, while
the Malay **kuda padi** is a short-legged horse for riding. **Dasparan**,
from the Khowan language of Pakistan, describes the mating of
horses and the Russian **nochoe** means the pasturing of horses for the
night. Persian has an extravagance of equine vocabulary:

zaru a horse that travels nimbly with long steps
mirjam a horse that makes the dirt fly when running
raji a horse returning tired from a journey only to be
   immediately dispatched upon another
rakl to strike a horse with the heel to make it gallop
zau' shaking the horse's rein to quicken the pace
shiyar riding a horse backwards and forwards to show it off to
   a buyer
safin a horse standing on three legs and touching the ground
   with the tip of its fourth hoof

Man's best friend

The Indians of Guatemala have a word, **nagual**, which describes an animal, chosen at birth, whose fate is believed to have a direct effect on the prosperity of its owner.

Hopping mad

The Kunwinjku of Australia use a range of words to describe the way in which kangaroos hop; in part this is because, from a distance, the easiest way to identify a particular type of kangaroo is by the way it moves. Thus **kanjedjme** is the hopping of a wallaroo, **kamawudme** is the hopping of a male Antilopine wallaroo, and **kadjalwahme** is the hopping of the female. **Kamurlbardme** is the hopping of a black wallaroo and **kalurlhlurlme** is the hopping of an agile wallaby.

False friends

ape (Italian) bee
anz (Arabic) wasp
bum (Arabic) owl
medusa (Spanish) jellyfish
slurp (Afrikaans) elephant's trunk
ukelele (Tongan) jumping flea

Shoo!

The Latin American **sape**, the German **husch** and the Pashto (of Afghanistan and Pakistan) **tsheghe tsheghe** are among the many similar-sounding words that mean 'shoo'. Other animal commands refer to particular creatures: Pashto **pishte pishte** is said when chasing cats away; **gja gja** is the Bulgar driving call to horses; **kur** is the Indonesian call to chickens to come to be fed; and **belekisi ontu** (Aukan, Suriname) is an insult hurled at a dog. The Malays are even more specific, with **song**, the command to an elephant to lift one leg, and **soh**, the cry to a buffalo to turn left.

Peacocks' tails

Many languages identify specific parts or attributes of animals for which there is no direct English equivalent. **Kauhaga moa** is the word used by Easter Islanders to designate the first and shortest claw of a chicken, while **candraka** in Tulu (India) is the eye pattern that appears on the feathers of a peacock's tail and **kannu** is the star in the feather. In several languages there are particular words for different types of animal excrement: monkey urine in the Guajá language (Brazil) is **kalukaluk-kaí**; the liquid part of chicken excrement in Ulwa (Nicaragua) is **daraba**; while in Persian the little bit of sweat and dung attached to a sheep's groin and tail is called **wazahat**.

Kissing and hissing

Other words describe the closely observed actions of animals, many of which we can instantly recognize:

mengais (Indonesian) to scratch on the ground with claws in search of food (generally used of a chicken)

apisik (Turkish) any animal holding its tail between its legs

maj u maj (Persian) kissing and licking (as a cat does to her kittens)

greann (Scottish Gaelic) the hair bristling as on an enraged dog

fahha (Arabic) the hissing of a snake

tau'ani (Cook Islands Maori) to squeal at one another while fighting (used of cats)

kikamu (Hawaiian) the gathering of fish about a hook that they hesitate to bite

alevandring (Danish) the migration of the eel

paarnguliaq (Inuit) a seal that has strayed and now can't find its breathing hole

Two Persian tricks

Tuti'i pas ayina is a person sitting behind a mirror who teaches a parrot to talk by making it believe that it is its own likeness seen in the mirror which is pronouncing the words. While **kalb** is the practice of imitating barking to induce dogs to respond and thus show whether a particular dwelling is inhabited or not.

Animal magnetism

Some animal words attract other meanings as well. Hausa of Nigeria uses **mesa** to mean both python and water hose, and **jak** both donkey and wheelbarrow. **Wukur** in Arabic signifies a bird of prey's nest

and an aircraft hangar and, intriguingly, **zamma** means both to put a bridle on a camel and to be supercilious. For the Wagiman of Australia **wanganyjarri** describes a green ants' nest and an armpit, while for the French **papillon** is both a butterfly and a parking ticket.

The flying squad

In Hopi, an Amerindian language, **masa'ytaka** is used to denote insects, aeroplanes, pilots; in fact, everything that flies except birds.

Tamed

Humans have rarely been content to let animals run wild and free; using them in one way or another has defined the relationship between two and four legs:

ch'illpiy (Quechuan, Peru) to mark livestock by cutting their ears

bolas (Spanish) two or three heavy balls joined by a cord used to entangle the legs of animals

oorxax (Khakas, Siberia) a wooden ring in the nose of a calf (to prevent it from suckling from its mother)

hundeskole (Danish) a dog-training school

Animal sounds

In Albanian, Danish, English, Hebrew and Polish, to name just a few languages, bees make a buzzing sound, and cats miaow. However, no language but English seems to think that owls go 'tu-whit, tu-woo' or a cockerel goes 'cock-a-doodle-doo'. And not everyone agrees about the birds and the bees either:

Birds
Arabic (Algeria): **twit twit**
Bengali: **cooho'koohoo**
Finnish: **tsirp tsirp**
Hungarian: **csipcsirip**
Korean: **ji-ji-bae-bae**
Norwegian: **kvirrevitt** or **pip-pip**

Bees
Afrikaans: **zoem-zoem**
Bengali: **bhonbhon**

Estonian: **summ-summ**
Japanese: **bunbun**
Korean: **boong-boong** or **wing-wing**

Cats
Indonesian: **ngeong**
Malay: **ngiau**
Nahuatl (Mexico): **tlatzomia**

Chicks
Albanian: **ciu ciu**
Greek: **ko-ko-ko**
Hungarian: **csip-csip**
Indonesian: **cip cip**
Quechuan (Peru): **tojtoqeyay**
Slovene: **čiv-čiv**
Thai: **jiap jiap**
Turkish: **cik cik**

Cockerels
Chinese: **gou gou**
French: **cocorico**
Italian: **chicchirichí**
Portuguese: **cocorococo**
Thai: **ake-e-ake-ake**

Cows
Bengali: **hamba**
Dutch: **boeh**
Hungarian: **bú**
Korean: **um-muuuu**
Nahuatl (Mexico): **choka**

Crows
French: **croa-croa**
Indonesian: **gagak**
Korean: **kka-ak-kka-ak**
Spanish: **cruaaac, cruaaac**
Swedish: **krax**
Thai: **gaa gaa**
Turkish: **gaaak, gaak**

Cuckoos
Japanese: **kakkou kakkou**
Korean: **ppu-kkook-ppu-kkook**
Turkish: **guguk, guguk**

Elephants
Finnish: **trööt** or **prööt**
Spanish (Chile): **prraaahhh, prrraaaahhh**
Thai: **pran pran**

Frogs
Afrikaans: **kwaak-kwaak**
Estonian: **krooks-krooks**
Munduruku (Brazil): **korekorekore**
Spanish (Argentina): **berp**

Goats
Nahuatl (Mexico): **choka**
Norwegian: **mae**
Quechuan (Peru): **jap'apeyay**
Russian: **mee**
Ukrainian: **me-me**

Hens
Turkish: **gut-gut-gudak**
Arabic (Algeria): **cout cout cout**
Rapa Nui (Easter Island): **kókokóko**

Owls
Korean: **buung-buung**
Norwegian: **uhu**
Russian: **ukh**
Swedish: **hoho**
Thai: **hook hook**

Pigs
Albanian: **hunk hunk**
Hungarian: **röf-röf-röf**
Japanese: **buubuu, boo boo boo**
Dutch: **knor-knor**

Sheep
Mandarin Chinese: **mieh mieh**
Portuguese: **meee meee**
Slovene: **bee-bee**
Vietnamese: **be-hehehe**
French: **bêê (h)**

Spellcheck nightmare

If only Scrabble allowed foreign words how much greater our wordscores could be:

3 consecutive vowels: **aaa** (Hawaiian) a lava tube

4 consecutive vowels: **jaaaarne** (Estonian) the edge of the ice; **kuuuurija** (Estonian) a moon explorer

6 consecutive vowels: **zaaiuien** (Dutch) onions for seeding; **ouaouaron** (Quebecois French) a bullfrog

7 consecutive vowels: **hääyöaie** (Finnish) – counting 'y' as a vowel – a plan for the wedding night

8 consecutive vowels: **hooiaioia** (Hawaiian) certified; **oueaiaaare** (Estonian) the edge of a fence surrounding a yard

5 consecutive consonants (and no vowels): **cmrlj** (Slovenian) a bumblebee

7 consecutive consonants: **razzvrkljati** (Slovenian) preparing the egg for baking, or making omelettes; **opskrbljivač** (Croatian) a supplier; **ctvrtkruh** (Czech) a quadrant

8 consecutive consonants: **angstschreeuw** (Dutch) a cry of fear; **varldsschlager** (Swedish) a worldwide music hit; **gvbrdgvnit** (Georgian) you tear us into pieces

11 consecutive consonants: **odctvrtvrstvit** (Czech) to remove a quarter of a layer

Whatever the Weather

chuntian hai'er lian, yi tian
bian san bian (*Chinese*)
*spring weather is like a child's face, changing
three times a day*

And the forecast is ...

Despite our obsession with the weather, the English language doesn't cover all the bases when it comes to precise observations of the natural world ...

serein (French) fine rain falling from a cloudless sky
imbat (Turkish) a daytime summer sea breeze
'inapoiri (Cook Islands Maori) a moonless night
wamadat (Persian) the intense heat of a still, sultry night
gumusservi (Turkish) moonlight shining on water
tojji (Tulu, India) the scum of water collected into bubbles
efterarsfarver (Danish) autumn colours

... though, inevitably, there are some local phenomena that we have to struggle harder to imagine:

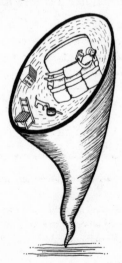

wilikoi (Hawaiian) substances that are gathered up in the centre of a whirlwind

isblink (Swedish) the luminous appearance of the horizon caused by reflection from ice

Meteorological metaphors

Our descriptions of the weather often use metaphors, such as raining cats and dogs, but some languages use the weather itself as the metaphor:

Schnee von gestern (German) yesterday's snow (water under the bridge)

huutaa tuuleen (Finnish) to shout to the wind (to do something that has no use)

aven solen har fläckar (Swedish) even the sun has got spots (no one is perfect)

snést někomu modré z nebe (Czech) to bring the blue down from the sky for someone (do anything to please them)

chap phar kah chap jil pa chu kha ray (Dzongkha, Bhutan) the rain falls yonder, but the drops strike here (indirect remarks hit the target)

xihuitl barq (Arabic) lightning without a downpour (a disappointment, a disillusionment or an unkept promise)

Those words for snow

The number of different Inuit words for snow has been the subject of endless debate, few people taking into account the fact that the now-offensive group name 'Eskimo' (from the French **Esquimaux**, derived from North American Algonquian and literally meaning 'eaters of raw flesh') covers a number of different language areas: Inuit in Greenland and Canada, Yupik in Eastern Siberia and Aleut in Alaska. Here is a selection of words for snow from some Inuit languages:

snow, **kaniktshaq**; no snow, **aputaitok**; to snow, **qanir**, **qanunge**, **qanugglir**; snowy weather, **nittaatsuq**, **qannirsuq**; to get fine snow or rain particles, **kanevcir**; first falling, **apingaut**; light falling, **qannialaag**; wet and falling, **natatgo naq**; in the air, falling, **qaniit**; feathery clumps of falling snow, **qanipalaat**; air thick with snow, **nittaalaq**; rippled surface of snow, **kaiyuglak**; light, deep enough for walking, **katiksugnik**; fresh without any ice, **kanut**; crusty, **sillik**; soft for travelling, **mauyasiorpok**; soft and deep where snowshoes are needed for travel, **taiga**; powder, **nutagak**; salty, **pokaktok**; wind-beaten, **upsik**; fresh, **nutaryuk**; packed, **aniu**; sharp, **panar**; crusty that breaks under foot, **karakartanaq**; rotten, slush on sea, **qinuq**; best for building an igloo, **pukaangajuq**; glazed in a thaw, **kiksrukak**; watery, **mangokpok**; firm (the easiest to cut, the warmest, the preferred), **pukajaw**; loose, newly fallen which cannot be used as it is, but can provide good building material when compacted, **ariloqaq**; for melting into water, **aniuk**; that a dog eats, **aniusarpok**; that can be broken through, **mauya**; floating on water, **qanisqineq**; for building, **auverk**; on clothes, **ayak**; beaten from clothes, **tiluktorpok**; much on clothes, **aputainnarowok**; crust, **pukak**; cornice, formation about to collapse, **navcaq**; on the boughs of trees, **qali**; blown indoors, **sullarniq**; snowdrift overhead and about to fall, **mavsa**; snowdrift that blocks something, **kimaugruk**; smoky drifting snow, **siqoq**; arrow-shaped snowdrift, **kaluto-ganiq**; newly drifting snow, **akelrorak**; space between drifts and obstruction, **anamana**, **anymanya**; snowstorm, **pirsuq**, **pirsirsursuaq**, **qux**; violent snowstorm, **igadug**; blizzard, **pirta**, **pirtuk**; avalanche, **sisuuk**, **aput sisurtuq**; to get caught in an avalanche, **navcite**.

There are also a large number of Inuit words for ice, covering everything from icicles through 'solidly frozen slush' to 'open pack ice in seawater'.

False friends

air (Indonesian) water, liquid, juice
blubber (Dutch) mud
shit (Persian) dust
nap (Hungarian) sun
sky (Norwegian) cloud
pi (Korean) rain

Highland mist

Either there is more weather in the cold, wet places of the world or people have more time to think about and define it. The Scots may not have as many words for snow as the Inuits, but they have a rich vocabulary for their generally cool and damp climate.

Dreich is their highly evocative word for a miserably wet day. Gentle rain or **smirr** might be falling, either in a **dribble** (drizzle) or in a **dreep** (steady but light rainfall). **Plowtery** (showery) weather may shift to a **gandiegow** (squall), a **pish-oot** (complete downpour), or a **thunder-plump** (sudden rainstorm accompanied by thunder and lightning). Any of these is likely to make the average walker feel **dowie** (downhearted) as they push on through the **slaister** (liquid bog) and **glaur** (mire), even if they're not yet **drookit** (soaked to the skin). The track in front of them will probably be covered with **dubs** (puddles), as the neighbouring **burn** (stream) grows into a fast-flowing **linn** (torrent).

The very next day the weather may be different again, and the walker beset by **blenter** (gusty wind). Or if it's **grulie** (unsettled), there's always the hope that it might turn out **leesome** (fair) with a lovely **pirl** (soft breeze). And then, after the next **plype** (sudden heavy shower), there may even be a **watergow** (faint rainbow). In deepest winter it will generally be **snell** (piercingly cold), and sometimes **fair jeelit** (icily so) among the **wreaths** (drifts) of snow.

For a precious few fair days in summer, there may even be a **simmer cowt** (heat haze), though the more austere will be relieved that the likelihood of discomfort remains high on account of the fierce-biting **mudges** (midges).

My underground oven

Riddles are found the world over. Here are some intriguing ones from Hawaii:

1 **ku'u punawai kau i ka lewa** my spring of water high up in the clouds

2 **ku'u wahi pu ko'ula i ka moana** my bundle of red sugarcane in the ocean

3 **ku'u wahi hale, 'ewalu o'a, ho'okahi pou** my house with eight rafters and one post

4 **ku'u imu kalua loa a lo'ik'i** my long underground oven

Answers

1 **niu** a coconut

2 **anuenue** a rainbow

3 **mamula** an umbrella

4 **he** the grave

Hearing Things

quien quiere ruido, compre un cochino (*Spanish*)
he that loves noise must buy a pig

Sound bites

The sounds of most of the words we use have little to do with their meanings. But there are exceptions in other languages, too. For best results try saying the words out loud:

ata-ata (Rapa Nui, Easter Island) to laugh
ba'a (Hausa, Nigeria) ridicule, mockery
baqbaq (Arabic) garrulous
bulubushile (Bemba, Congo and Zambia) a stammer or lisp
capcap (Maltese) to clap
chopchop (Chamorro, Guam, USA) to suck
cizir cizir (Turkish) with a sizzling noise
karkara (Arabic) to rumble (of a stomach)
kekek-kekek (Malay) to giggle
kitikiti (Tulu, India) the ticking of a watch; or giggling, tittering

pes pes (Pashto, Afghanistan and Pakistan) whispering
pshurr (Albanian) to urinate, to wet one's clothes
raxxax (Maltese) to drizzle
ringongo (Gilbertese, Kiribati) to snore
taptap (Maltese) to patter

yuyurungul (Yindiny, Australia) the noise of a snake sliding through the grass

xiaoxiao (Chinese) the whistling and pattering of rain or wind

zonk zonk (Turkish) to throb terribly

Making a splash

Local experience shapes local language. The Tulu people of India, for example, have a fine array of evocative, specific words to do with water: **gulum** describes a stone falling into a well; **gulugulu** is filling a pitcher with water; **caracara** is spurting water from a pump; **budubudu** is bubbling, gushing water; **jalabala** is bubbling or boiling water; **salasala** is pouring water; while **calacala** describes the action of children wading through water as they play.

Ding dong

The sound of an altogether noisier culture can be heard in Indonesian: **kring** is the sound of a bicycle bell; **dentang**, cans being hit repeatedly; **reat-reot**, the squeaking of a door; **ning-nong**, the ringing of a doorbell; **jedar-jedor**, a door banging repeatedly. But there are gentler moments, too: **kecipak-kecipung** is hands splashing water in a rhythm, while **desus** is a quiet and smooth sound as of someone farting but not very loudly.

Chirping cuckoos

The Basques of the Pyrenees also use highly expressive words. You might recognize such terms as **kuku** (a cuckoo), **miau** (miaou), **mu** (moo), **durrunda** (thunder), **zurrumurru** (a whisper) and **urtzintz** (to sneeze), but could you guess the meaning of these?

thu	to spit
milikatu	to lick
tchiuka	to chirp
chichtu	to whistle
uhurritu	to howl
chehatu	to chew
karruskatu	to gnaw

False friends

rang (Chinese) to yell, shout
boo (Latin) to cry out, resound
hum (Ainu, Japan) sound, feeling
rumore (Italian) noise
bum (Turkish) bang

Sounds Japanese

The Japanese can be equally imitative: **shikushiku** is to cry continuously while sniffling, and **zeizei** is the sound of air being forced through the windpipe when one has a cold or respiratory illness. We can hear perhaps a gathering of Japanese women in **kusukusu**, to giggle or titter, especially in a suppressed voice; and of men in **geragera**, a belly laugh. Moving from the literal to the more imaginative, the Japanese have **sa**, the sound of a machine with the switch on, idling quietly; **sooay sooay**, fish swimming; **susu**, the sound of air passing continuously through a small opening.

Gitaigo describes a more particular Japanese concept: words that try to imitate not just sounds, but states of feeling. So **gatcha gatcha** describes an annoying noise; **harahara** refers to one's reaction to something one is directly involved in; and **ichaicha** is used of a couple engaging in a public display of affection viewed as unsavoury by passers-by. Mimicry of feelings extends to descriptions of the way we see: so **jirojiro** is to stare in fascination; **tekateka** is the shiny appearance of a smooth (often cheap-looking) surface; **pichapicha** is splashing water; and **kirakira** is a small light that blinks repeatedly.

Sounds familiar

Not all words about sound are imitative; or perhaps it's just that things strike the ear differently in other parts of the world:

bagabaga (Tulu, India) the crackling of a fire

desir (Malay) the sound of sand driven by the wind

faamiti (Samoan) to make a squeaking sound by sucking air past the lips in order to gain the attention of a dog or children

riman (Arabic) the sound of a stone thrown at a boy

ghiqq (Persian) the sound made by a boiling kettle

kertek (Malay) the sound of dry leaves or twigs being trodden underfoot

lushindo (Bemba, Congo and Zambia) the sound of footsteps

nyangi (Yindiny, Australia) any annoying noise

yuyin (Chinese) the remnants of sound which remain in the ears of the hearer

Top ten

In terms of numbers of speakers, the top ten world languages are as follows:

1 Mandarin 1,000+ million
2 English 508 million
3 Hindi 497 million
4 Spanish 342 million
5 Russian 277 million
6 Arabic 246 million
7 Bengali 211 million
8 Portuguese 191 million
9 Malay–Indonesian 159 million
10 French 129 million

Seeing Things

cattiva è quella lana che non si
puo tingere *(Italian)*
it is a bad cloth that will take no colour

Colourful language

We might well think that every language has a word for every colour, but this isn't so. Nine languages distinguish only between black and white. In Dan, for example, which is spoken in New Guinea, people talk in terms of things being either **mili** (darkish) or **mola** (lightish).

Twenty-one languages have distinct words for black, red and white only; eight have those colours plus green; then the sequence in which additional colours are brought into languages is yellow, with a further eighteen languages, then blue (with six) and finally brown (with seven).

Across the spectrum

As with colours, so with the rainbow. The Bassa language of Liberia identifies only two colours: **ziza** (red/orange/yellow) and **hui** (green/blue/purple) in their spectrum. The Shona of Zimbabwe describe four: **cipsuka** (red/orange), **cicena** (yellow and yellow-green), **citema** (green-blue) and **cipsuka** again (the word also represents the purple end of the spectrum). It is just Europeans and the Japanese who pick out seven colours: red, orange, yellow, green, blue, indigo and violet.

Welsh blues

The Welsh for blue is **glas**, as in the expression **yng nglas y dydd**, in the blue of the day (the early morning). But **glas** is a hard-working word. It's also used in the expression **gorau glas** (blue best), to mean to do one's best, and, changing tack rather dramatically, it appears as **glas wen** (blue smile), a smile that is insincere and mocking. In Welsh literature, **glas** is a colour that is somewhere between green, blue and grey; it also has poetic meanings of both youth and death.

False friends

blank (German) shiny
hell (German) clear, bright, light
cafe (Quechuan, Peru) brown

Thai dress code

Thais believe that if they dress in a certain colour each day it will bring them good luck. The code is: Monday, yellow (**lueang**); Tuesday, pink (**chom poo**); Wednesday, green (**kiaw**); Thursday, orange (**som**); Friday, blue (**nam ngem**); Saturday, purple (**muang**); Sunday, red (**daeng**). Black (**dam**) is not lucky for conservative people and is reserved for funerals; unless you are young, in which case it's seen as edgy and sophisticated.

Colour-coded

We can be green with envy, see red, or feel a bit blue. Colours have a strong symbolic force, but not everyone agrees on what they stand for:

Red
makka na uso (Japanese) a deep red (outright) lie
aka no tannin (Japanese) a red (total) stranger
film a luci rosse (Italian) a red (blue) film
romanzo rosa (Italian) a pink (romantic) story
vyspat se do červena/růžova (Czech) to sleep oneself into the red (have had a good night's sleep)

Yellow
jaune d'envie (French) yellow (green) with envy
gelb vor Eifersucht werden (German) to become yellow with jealousy
kiroi koi (Japanese) a yellow (particularly screeching) scream
gul och blå (Swedish) yellow and blue (black and blue)

Black

svartsjuk (Swedish) black ill (jealousy)

hara guroi (Japanese) black stomach (wicked)

être noir (French) to be black (drunk)

mustasukkainen (Finnish) wearing black socks (jealous)

White

andare in bianco (Italian) to go into the white (to have no success with someone romantically)

ak akce kara gun icindir (Turkish) white money for a black day (savings for a rainy day)

un mariage blanc (French) a white marriage (a marriage of convenience)

obléci bílý kabát (archaic Czech) to put on the white coat (to join the army)

Blue

aoiki toiki (Japanese) sighing with blue breath (suffering)

blau sein (German) to be blue (drunk)

en être bleu (French) to be in the blue (struck dumb)

aoku naru (Japanese) blue with fright

blått öga (Swedish) blue eye (black eye)

modré pondělí (Czech) blue Monday (a Monday taken as holiday after the weekend)

Green

al verde (Italian) in the green (short of cash)

vara pa gron kvist (Swedish) as rich as green (wealthy)

langue verte (French) green language (slang)

darse un verde (Spanish) to give oneself greens (to tuck into one's food)

aotagai (Japanese) to buy green rice fields (to employ college students prematurely)

Polyglossary

Two countries, Papua New Guinea with over 850 languages and Indonesia with around 670, are home to a quarter of the world's languages. If we add the seven countries that each possess more than two hundred languages (Nigeria 410, India 380, Cameroon 270, Australia 250, Mexico 240, Zaire 210, Brazil 210), the total comes to almost 3,500; which is to say that more than half of the world's spoken languages come from just nine countries.

If we look at it in terms of continents, North, Central and South America have around one thousand spoken languages, which is about 15 per cent; Africa has around 30 per cent; Asia a bit over 30 per cent; and the Pacific somewhat under 20 per cent. Europe is by far the least diverse, having only 3 per cent of the world's languages.

Number Crunching

c'est la goutte d'eau qui fait
déborder le vase *(French)*
*it's the drop of water that makes the vase
overflow*

Countdown

You might expect words to get longer as numbers get bigger, so perhaps it's a surprise to find that in some languages the words for single digits are a real mouthful. In the Ona-Shelknam language of the Andes, for example, eight is **ningayuneng aRvinelegh**. And in Athabaskan Koyukon (an Alaskan language) you need to get right through **neelk'etoak'eek'eelek'eebedee'oane** to register the number seven.

Vital statistics

The world's vocabulary of numbers moves from the precise . . .

parab (Assyrian, Middle East) five-sixths
halvfemte (Danish) four and a half
lakh (Hindustani) one hundred thousand

. . . to the vague:

tobaiti (Machiguengan, Peru) any quantity above four
mpusho (Bemba, Congo and Zambia) any unit greater than the number ten
birkacinci (Turkish) umpteen

Counting in old China

From the very biggest to the very smallest, the Ancient Chinese were highly specific in their delineation of numbers, from:

tsai 100 trillion
cheng 10 trillion
chien a trillion
kou 100 billion
jang 10 billion
pu / tzu a billion
kai 100 million
ching 10 million

right down to:

ch'ien one tenth
fen one hundredth
li one thousandth
hao one ten-thousandth
ssu one hundred-thousandth
hu one millionth
wei one ten-millionth
hsien one hundred-millionth
sha one billionth
ch'en one ten-billionth

Double-digit growth

Counting in multiples of ten probably came from people totting up items on their outspread fingers and thumbs. Some cultures, however, have approached matters rather differently. The Ancient Greeks rounded things off to sixty (for their low numbers) and 360 (for their high numbers) and speakers of old Germanic used to say 120 to mean many. The Yuki of Northern California counted in multiples of eight (being the space between their two sets of fingers) and rounded off high numbers at sixty-four. Some Indian tribes in California based their multiples on five and ten; others liked four as it expressed North, South, East and West; others six because it added to those directions the worlds above and below ground.

Magic numbers

Different cultures give different significance to different numbers. Western traditions offer the five senses and the seven sins, among other groupings. Elsewhere we find very different combinations. The following list is drawn from the Tulu language of India unless otherwise stated:

Three
tribhuvara the three worlds: heaven, earth and hell
trivarga the three human objects: love, duty and wealth

Four
nalvarti the four seasons

Five
pancabhuta the five elements: earth, air, fire, water and ether
pancaloha the five chief metals: gold, silver, copper, iron and
    lead

pancavarna the five colours: white, black, red, yellow and green

pancamahapataka the five greatest sins: murdering a Brahman, stealing gold, drinking alcohol, seducing the wife of one's spiritual mentor, and associating with a person who has committed such sins

pancavadya the five principal musical instruments: lute, cymbals, drum, trumpet and oboe

Six

liuqin (Chinese) the six relations (father, mother, elder brothers, younger brothers, wife and children)

Seven

haft rang (Persian) the seven colours of the heavenly bodies: Saturn, black; Jupiter, brown; Mars, red; the Sun, yellow; Venus, white; Mercury, blue; and the Moon, green

Eight

ashtabhoga the eight sources of enjoyment: habitation, bed, clothing, jewels, wife, flower, perfumes and betel-leaf/areca nut

Nine

sembako (Indonesian) the nine basic commodities that people need for everyday living: rice, flour, eggs, sugar, salt, cooking oil, kerosene, dried fish and basic textiles

Ten

dah ak (Persian) the ten vices – named after the tyrant Zahhak who was notorious for ten defects of body or mind: ugliness, shortness of stature, excessive pride, indecency, gluttony, scurrility, cruelty, hastiness, falsehood and cowardice

Expressed numerically

Specific numbers are also used in some colloquial phrases:

mettre des queues aux zeros (French) to add tails to noughts
(to overcharge)

siete (Spanish, Central America) seven (a right-angled tear)

Mein Rad hat eine Acht (German) my bike has an eight (a
buckled wheel)

se mettre sur son trente et un (French) to put yourself on
your thirty-one (to get all dressed up)

ein Gesicht wie 7 Tage Regenwetter haben (German) to
have a face like seven days of rain (a long face)

Kissing time

The adult understanding of the French number **soixante-neuf**
(69) is well known. Less familiar is the other meaning of **quatre-
vingt-huit** (88) – a kiss.

Take your time

Not everyone sees time in terms of past, present and future. The Kipsigis of the Nile region have three types of past tense: today's past, yesterday's past and the distant past. Several American Indian languages divide the past tense into the recent past, remote past and mythological past; other languages have different definitions:

pal (Hindi) a measure of time equal to twenty-four seconds
ghari (Hindi) a small space of time (twenty-four minutes)
tulat (Malay) the third day hence
xun (Chinese) a period of ten days (in a month) or a decade (in someone's life)
jam karet (Indonesian) rubber time (an indication that meetings may not necessarily start on time)

Can't say exactly when

In Hindi, the word for yesterday, **kal**, is the same as that for tomorrow (only the tense of the attached verb tells you which). And in Punjabi **parson** means either the day before yesterday or the day after tomorrow.

Time of day

Around the world different cultures have created highly specific loosely clock-related vocabulary that divides up the day. The Zarma people of Western Africa use **wete** to cover mid-morning (between nine and ten); the Chinese **wushi** is from eleven to one; and the Hausa (of Nigeria) **azahar** takes in the period from one-thirty to around three. The Samoan word **afiafi** covers both late afternoon and evening, from about 5 p.m. till dark. They call the period right after sunset **afiafi po**; this is then followed after a couple of hours by **po**, the dead of night. Of the various expressions for dusk, perhaps the most evocative is the French **entre chien et loup** – literally, between the dog and the wolf.

Elevenses

Dutch (and other Germanic languages) confusingly uses **half twaalf** for 11.30. While in Africa they are more long-winded for this specific time of day:

baguo gbelleng pie ne yeni par miti lezare ne pie (Dagaari Dioula, Burkina Faso)

isikhathi yisigamu emva kwehora leshumi nanye (Zulu)

metsotso e mashome a meraro ka mora hora ya leshome le motso e mong (Sesotho, Southern Africa)

Shouting the distance

Krosa is Sanskrit for a cry, and thus has come to mean the distance over which a man's call can be heard, roughly two miles. In the central forests of Sri Lanka calculations of distance are also made by sound: a dog's bark indicates a quarter of a mile; a cock's crow something more; and a **hoo** is the space over which a man can be heard when shouting the word at the highest pitch of his voice. While in the Yakut language of Siberia, **kiosses** represents a specific distance calculated in terms of the time it takes to cook a piece of meat.

Tip to toe

Parts of the body have long been used to define small distances – the foot in the imperial system of measuring, for example. The Zarma people of Western Africa find the arm much more useful: **kambe kar** is the length of the arm from the elbow to the tip of the middle finger and **gande** is the distance between two outstretched arms. Elsewhere we find:

dos (Hmong, China) from the thumb tip to the middle-finger tip

muku (Hawaiian) from the fingers of one hand to the elbow of the opposite arm when it is extended

sejengkal (Malay) the span between the tips of the stretched thumb and little finger

dangkal (Kapampangan, Philippines) between thumb and forefinger

The Micmac calendar

The Mikmawisimk language of the Micmac Indians is spoken by some eight thousand people in Canada and the USA. Their twelve months all have highly evocative names:

English	Mikmawisimk	Literal translation
January	**Punamujuikús**	the cod are spawning
February	**Apunknajit**	the sun is powerful
March	**Siwkewikús**	maple sugar
April	**Penamuikús**	birds lay eggs
May	**Etquljuikús**	frogs are croaking
June	**Nipnikús**	foliage is most verdant
July	**Peskewikús**	birds are moulting
August	**Kisikwekewikús**	it's ripening time
September	**Wikumkewikús**	it's moose-calling time
October	**Wikewikús**	our animals are fat and tame
November	**Keptekewikús**	the rivers are about to freeze
December	**Kiskewikús**	chief moon

False friends

fart (Turkish) excess or exaggeration
dim (Welsh) zero
age (Hindi and Urdu, Pakistan) in the future
beast (Persian) twenty
slut (Swedish) end or finish
tilt (Cantonese) one-third

Caribou calendar

Similar charmingly named months make up the various Inuit calendars. January is **siqinnaarut**, the month when the sun returns; February is **qangattaarjuk**, referring to the sun getting higher and higher in the sky; March is **avunniit**, when premature baby seals are born: some make it, some freeze to death; April is **natsijjat**, the proper month for seal pups to be born; May is **tirigluit**, when bearded seals are born; June is **manniit**, when the birds are laying eggs; July is **saggaruut**, the sound of rushing water as the rivers start to run; August is **akulliruut**, when the summer has come and the caribous' thick hair has been shed; September is **amiraijaut**, when the caribou hair is neither too thin nor too thick but just right for making into clothing; October is **ukialliruut**, when the caribou antlers lose their covers; November is **tusaqtuut**, when the ice forms and people can travel to see other people and get news; December is **taujualuk**, a very dark month.

Tea time

Tea is a fundamental part of Chinese culture, so it's no surprise to find that there's an elaborate calendar relating to the growth and preparation of it:

Chinese	Literal translation	Western Calendar
Li Chun	spring starts	5 February
Yushui	the rains come	19 February
Jingzhe	insects wake up	5 March
Chunfen	spring equinox	20 March
Qingming	clear and bright	5 April
Guyu	grain rain	20 April
Lixia	summer starts	5 May

Chinese	Literal translation	Western Calendar
Xiaoman	grains fill out	21 May
Mangzhong	the grain is in ear	6 June
Xiazhu	summer solstice	21 June
Xiaoshu	little heat	7 July
Dashu	big heat	23 July
Liqiu	autumn starts	7 August
Chushu	limit to food	23 August
Bailu	white dew	8 September
Qiufen	autumn equinox	23 September
Hanlu	cold dew	8 October
Shuangjiang	frost descends	23 October
Lidong	winter starts	7 November
Xiaoxue	little snow	22 November
Daxue	big snow	7 December
Dongzhi	winter solstice	21 December
Xiohan	little cold	6 January
Dahan	big cold	26 January

Halcyon days

In 2002 President Saparmurat Niyazov of Turkmenistan decided to rename both the months of the year and the days of the week. Some months were to take the names of heroes of Turkmenistan's past, but January was to become **Turkmenbashi**, after the president's official name ('Head of all the Turkmen'). In response to his suggestion that April should become known as 'Mother', one of his supporters suggested that instead it should be named after the president's mother, **Gurbansoltan-eje**. The president heeded this advice.

The days of the week were also renamed: Monday became Major (main or first) Day; Tuesday, Young Day; Wednesday, Favourable Day; Thursday, Blessed Day; Friday remained as it was; but Saturday became Spiritual Day; and Sunday, Rest Day.

Revolutionary

Turkmenistan is not the only country to consider changing the months of the year at a single stroke. In 1793 the newly established French republic abandoned the Gregorian calendar in favour of a new, 'rational' calendar. It lasted thirteen years, until abolished by Napoleon in 1806.

Each season was divided into three months, and the name of the months in each season shared a common word ending.

Printemps *(spring)*
Germinal seeds sprouting

Floréal flowering
Prairial meadow

Eté *(summer)*
Messidor harvest
Thermidor heat
Fructidor fruit

Automne *(autumn)*
Vendémiaire vintage
Brùmaire fog
Frimaire sleet

Hiver *(winter)*
Nivôse snow
Pluviôse rain
Ventôse winds

These months quickly became nicknamed by the British as Showery, Flowery, Bowery, Wheaty, Heaty, Sweety, Slippy, Nippy, Drippy, Freezy, Wheezy and Sneezy.

Stages of the Hawaiian moon

The Hawaiians in earlier times named each of the thirty nights of a lunar month. The first night was called **hilo**, to twist, because the moon was like a twisted thread. The second was **hoaka**, a crescent. The third was **ku-kahi**, the day of a very low tide. The subsequent days described rough seas, light after moonset or days suitable for fishing with a torch. On the eleventh night, **huna**, the sharp points of the crescent were lost. On the twelfth, **mohalu**, the moon began to round. This was a favoured night for planting flowers; it was believed they would be round too. The thirteenth night was **hua**, the egg; the fourteenth, **akua**, the night of the perfectly rounded moon. On the sixteenth night, **mahea-lani**, the moon began to wane. More named days of rough seas followed until the twenty-ninth night, **mauli**, meaning that the last of the moon was visible. **Muku**, the thirtieth night, literally meant 'cut off' as the moon had disappeared.

A time for celebration

njepi (Balinese, Indonesia) a national holiday during which everyone is silent

Process of elimination

Not just words, but languages themselves change endlessly, some to the point where they go out of use altogether (on average one language a fortnight). Out of the (roughly speaking) 6,800 languages that comprise the global range, some recent victims have included Catawba (Massachusetts), Eyak (Alaska) and Livonian (Latvia). Many are from the jungles of Papua New Guinea, which still has more languages than any other country.

Others that run an imminent risk of extinction are: Abkhaz (Turkey/Georgia); Aleut (Alaska); Archi (Daghestan); British Romany; Apurina/Monde/Purubora/Mekens/ Ayuru/Xipaya (Brazil); Brapu (Papua New Guinea); Southern Chaco/Chorote/Nivacle/Kadiweu (South America); Diyari (South Australia); Eastern Penan (Sarawak and Brunei); Gamilaraay (New South Wales); Goemai (Nigeria); Guruntum (Nigeria); Iquito (Peru); Jawoyn (Southern Arnhem Land); Jiwarli/Thalanji (Western Australia); Khumi Chin (Western Myanmar); Sandaun (Papua New Guinea); Sasak (Eastern Indonesia); Lakota (The Plains, America); Maku (East Timor); Ngamini (South Australia); Rongga (Flores, Indonesia); Uspanteko and Sakapulteko (Guatamala); Takana and Reyesano (Bolivia); Tofa (Siberia); Tundra Nenets (Arctic Russia and Northwestern Siberia); Uranina (Peru); Vedda (Sri Lanka); Vures (Vanuatu).

What's in a Name?

ming bu zheng; yan bu shun
(Chinese)
*if the name is not right, the words cannot
be appropriate*

Angry bumblebees

Most first names, if not derived from myth, place, flower or surnames, have a specific meaning. **Patrick**, for example, means noble, from the Latin **patricius**. **Naomi** means 'pleasant' in Hebrew, while the Irish Gaelic **Kevin** literally means 'comely birth'. More unusual meanings of names from around the world include the following (m stands for a male name; f for female):

Astell (m)	sacred cauldron of the gods (Manx)
Delisha (f)	happy and makes others happy (Arabic)
Ebru (f)	eyebrow (Turkish)
Farooq (m)	he who distinguishes truth from falsehood (Arabic)
Fenella (f)	fair shoulder (Manx)
Lama (f)	with dark lips (Arabic)
Matilda (f)	strength in battle (German)
Xicohtencatl (m)	angry bumblebee (Nahuatl, Mexico)
Xiao-Xiao (f)	morning sorrow (Chinese)

Eyes like hard porridge

A number of particularly evocative names are to be found in different parts of Africa. Sometimes they refer to pregnancy or birth:

U-Zenzo (m)	things happened in the womb (Ndebele, Southern Africa)
Anindo (m)	mother slept a lot during pregnancy (Luo, Kenya)
Arogo (m)	mother nagged a lot during pregnancy (Luo, Kenya)
Ige (f)	born feet first (Yoruba, Nigeria)
Amadi (m)	seemed destined to die at birth (Yoruba, Nigeria)
Haoniyao (m)	born at the time of a quarrel (Swahili)

. . . to prophecy or destiny:

Amachi (f)	who knows what God has brought us through this child (Ibo, Nigeria)
U-Linda (f)	mind the village until the father's return (Ndebele, Southern Africa)
Nnamdi (m)	my father is alive (when thought to be a reincarnation of his grandfather) (Ibo, Nigeria)
Sankofa (f)	one must return to the past in order to move forward (Akan, Ghana)

. . . to appearance or behaviour:

Chiku (f)	chatterer (Swahili)
Masopakyindi (m)	eyes like hard porridge (Nyakyusa, Tanzania)
Masani (f)	has a gap between the front teeth (Buganda, Uganda)

. . . or to the parental reaction:

U-Thokozile (f) we are happy to have a child (Ndebele, Southern Africa)

Abeni (f) we asked for her and behold we got her (Yoruba, Nigeria)
Guedado (m) wanted by nobody (Fulani, Mali)
Anele (f) enough (given to a last born) (Xhosa, South Africa)

Silent foreigners

Czechs describe people from outside their country in intriguing caricature. Originally all foreigners were called **Němec** (from the adjective **němý** meaning 'mute'); now the suggestion that outsiders are deprived of speech applies specifically to Germans, whose country is known as **Německo**. Hungary in Czech used to be **Uhersko**, and a Hungarian **Uher**, literally, a pimple.

The Italians, meanwhile, are called **makaróni**, for obvious reasons; while Australians are known as **protinožcí**, meaning 'legs placed in an opposite direction', as they would be on the other side of the globe. Other cheerfully frank generalizations include: **opilý jako Dán**, to be as drunk as a Dane; **zmizet po anglicku**, to disappear like an Englishman; and when the Czechs *really* don't understand something, they say **to pro mně španělská vesnice**, it's all a Spanish village to me.

False friends

handel (Polish and Dutch) trade

liszt (Hungarian) flour

berlin (Wagiman, Australia) shoulder

bengal (Malay) temporarily deaf or stubborn

malta (Italian) mortar

bach (Welsh) cottage

pele (Samoan) pack of playing cards

Skin and buttocks

Just for the record, and to avoid confusion abroad, here are the meanings of a variety of English names when written in other languages:

adam (Arabic) skin
alan (Indonesian) comedian
alf (Arabic) thousand, millennium
anna (Arabic) moans and groans
calista (Portuguese) chiropodist
camilla (Spanish) stretcher

cilla (Zarma, Nigeria) basket
doris (Bajan, Barbados) police van

eliza (Basque) church

eve (Rapa Nui, Easter Island) buttocks

fay (Zarma, Nigeria) divorce

fred (Swedish, Danish and Norwegian) peace

jim (Korean) baggage

kim (Ainu, Japan) mountain

kylie (Dharug, Australia) boomerang

laura (Greek) group of monks' huts

luke (Chinese) traveller

marianna (Italian) accomplice who tells a gambler the cards held by other players

sara (Hausa, Nigeria) snakebite

sid (Arabic) plaster

susan (Thai) cemetery

vera (Italian) wedding ring

First person singular

Ben in Turkish, **Ami** in Bengali, **Fi** in Welsh, **Jo** in Catalan, **Mimi** in Swedish, **Mama** in Sinhala (Sri Lanka) and **Man** in Wolof (Senegal and Gambia) all mean I.

Speaking in tongues

British first names crop up as the names of languages, too:

Alan (Georgia); Ali (Central Africa); Dan (Ivory Coast); Dido (Russia); Karen (Myanmar and Thailand); Kim (Chad); Laura (Indonesia); Mae (Vanuatu); Maria (Papua New Guinea and India); Pam (Cameroon); Ron (Nigeria); Sara (Chad); Sonia (Papua New Guinea); Uma (Indonesia); Zaza (Iran).

And equally intriguing to English ears may be:

Afar (Ethiopia); Alas (Indonesia); Anus (Indonesia); Bare (Venezuela); Bats (Georgia); Bench (Ethiopia); Bile (Nigeria); Bit (Laos); Bum (Cameroon); Darling (Australia); Day (Chad); Doe (Tanzania); Eton (Vanuatu/Cameroon); Even (Russia); Ewe (Niger-Congo); Fang (Western Africa); Fox (North American); Fur (Sudan); Ham (Nigeria); Hermit (Papua New Guinea: extinct); Logo (Congo); Mango (Chad); Miao (South-East Asia); Moore (Burkina Faso); Mum (Papua New Guinea); Noon (Senegal); Pear (Cambodia); Poke (Congo); Puma (Nepal); Quiche (Guatemala).

Grand capital of the world

The capital of Thailand is abbreviated by all Thais to Krung Thep, and referred to as Bangkok, meaning literally 'grove of the wild plums'. But, bearing in mind that there are no spaces between words in written Thai, its full correct name is:

Krungthephphramahanakhonbowonratanakosinmahinthara yuthayamahadilokphiphobnovpharadradchataniburiromudo msantisug

meaning: City of Angels, Great City and Residence of the Emerald Buddha, Impregnable City of the God Indra, Grand Capital of the World, Endowed with Nine Precious Gems, Abounding in Enormous Royal Palaces which resemble the Heavenly Abode where reigns the Reincarnated God, a City given by Indra and built by Vishnukarm.

It rather leaves the Welsh

Llanfairpwllgwyngyllgogerychwyrndrobwillantysilioogofgoch

(meaning St Mary's Church by the pool of the white hazel trees, near the rapid whirlpool, by the red cave of the Church of St Tysilio) in the shade.

A to Y

At the other end of the scale are three places called **A** (in Denmark, Norway and Sweden), and two more, in Alaska and France, called **Y**.